PETER WALKER AND PARTNERS

PETER WALKER AND PARTNERS

LANDSCAPE ARCHITECTURE:

DEFINING THE CRAFT

First published in the United Kingdom in 2005 by
Thames & Hudson Ltd,
181A High Holborn,
London WC1V 7QX

www.thamesandhudson.com

Book concept and production by ORO editions
www.oroeditions.com

British Library Cataloguing-in-Publication Data
A catalogue record for this book is available from the British Library

ISBN-13:   978-0-500-34207-7
ISBN-10:   0-500-34207-5

Printed and bound in China by Global PSD

CONTENTS

PAST WORK

THE FIRM OF PETER WALKER AND PARTNERS (PWP) IS PART OF THE POSTWAR HISTORY OF LANDSCAPE ARCHITECTURE BEGINNING WITH THE TEACHING AND PRACTICE OF STANLEY WHITE AND HIDEO SASAKI. SASAKI'S INSIGHT CONNECTED THE EARLY DEFINING PRACTICE OF FREDERICK LAW OLMSTED AND HIS FOLLOWERS WITH THE SCALE OF THE TASKS POSED BY THE IMMENSE POSTWAR EXPANSION, FIRST IN THE UNITED STATES AND THEN THROUGHOUT THE WESTERN WORLD. IT WAS CLEAR TO THE YOUNG SASAKI THAT ONLY THOSE OFFICE ORGANIZATIONS COMBINING PLANNING AND DESIGN AND DEDICATED TO COLLABORATION WOULD BE ABLE TO ENGAGE THE MULTITUDE OF PROBLEMS THAT WOULD CHARACTERIZE THE LAST HALF OF THE TWENTIETH CENTURY. THEIR OFFICES WOULD REESTABLISH, REDESIGN, AND REDEFINE THE FIELD OF LANDSCAPE ARCHITECTURE—ITS PURPOSES, ITS PRACTICES, AND ITS ART. ORIGINATING IN DIFFERENT OFFICE ORGANIZATIONS OVER THE PAST FORTY YEARS, A SERIES OF PROJECTS MARKS THE DEVELOPMENT OF THE EXPERIENCE AND SKILL THAT FIND EXPRESSION IN RECENT WORK BY PWP. FREQUENTLY HONORED IN THEIR OWN RIGHT, THESE PROJECTS CONSTITUTE OUR CONTRIBUTION TO THE CRAFT OF LANDSCAPE ARCHITECTURE AND THE FUND OF KNOWLEDGE WE USE IN PRACTICE TODAY.

11

12

top
Alice in Wonderland
Central Park
New York, New York

middle
Upjohn Corporation
World Headquarters
Kalamazoo, Michigan

bottom
Concord Pavilion
Concord, California

top
Foothill College
Los Altos Hills, California   *middle*
Stanford University fountain   *Sidney Walton Park*
Palo Alto, California   *San Francisco, California*   *bottom*
Alcoa Plaza   *Security Pacific National Bank*   *Fashion Island Center*
San Francisco, California   *Los Angeles, California*   *Newport Beach, California*

14

Mountain View Shoreline Park
Mountain View, California

IBM West Coast
Programming Center
Santa Teresa, California

Crocker Plaza
San Francisco, Ca'ifornia

Weyerhaeuser Headquarters
Tacoma, Washington

20

University Park
Irvine, California

22

top
Cambridge Roof Garden
Cambridge, Massachusetts

middle
Marlborough Street Roof Garden
Boston, Massachusetts

bottom
Necco Garden
Massachusetts Institute
of Technology
Cambridge, Massachusetts

Portland Medical Center
Portland, Oregon

24

Tanner Fountain
Harvard University
Cambridge, Massachusetts

Burnett Park
Fort Worth, Texas

top
Herman Miller Regional Center
Rockland, California

middle
IBM Clearlake
Houston, Texas

bottom
Centrum Plaza
Redwood City, California

right
Hotel Kempinski
Munich Airport Center
Munich, Germany

28

IBM Solana
Westlake/Southlake, Texas

top
IBM sales center,
Spring, Winter
Solana main entry

middle
Parterre
IBM complex entrance
Allée and canal

bottom
Westin Hotel
Town Center
Stream and lake

right
IBM Solana fountain

30

Town Center
Costa Mesa,
California

top
South Coast Performing Arts Plaza
Opera arrival garden
Town Center Park

middle
Opera arrival garden
IBM Regional Headquarters with
sculpture by Aiko Miyawaki
Bollards at IBM Tower Plaza

bottom
Repertory theater terrace
Arrival plaza
Dining terrace

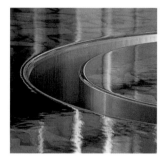

*IBM Plaza
Costa Mesa,
California*

32

IBM Japan Makuhari Building   *left*   *middle*   *right*
Makuhari, Japan   *Datum line of light*   *IBM Binary Garden*   *Water arrival garden*

Library Walk
University of California,
San Diego

	top	bottom	right
Toyota Municipal Museum of Art	Intimate sculpture garden	Iris bog and air fountain	The larch grove in the intimate
Toyota City, Japan	Monumental sculpture garden	Air fountain at dusk	sculpture garden

*Aerial view of reforestation
at Longacres Wetlands Park*

*Boeing Corporate
Administrative Center
Longacres Wetlands Park
Renton, Washington*

above
Stone and moss mountains
in ryokan garden

Conference Center
Nishi Harima, Japan

top
Nishi Harima Conference Center
Nishi Harima, Japan
Children at stone dam
Ryokan garden
Snake stream in bamboo grove

middle
Principal Mutual Life Plaza
Des Moines, Iowa
Park
Stage with mist fountain
Aerial view of paving

bottom
Principal Mutual Life Plaza
Des Moines, Iowa
Transparent wall and stair with
historic headquarters beyond
Lantern wall
Park with stone benches

Central Train Station Plaza
Muragame, Japan

left
Stone bollards at train station

middle
Plaza with rain fountain

right
Rain fountain at dusk

41

Oyama Training Center
Oyama, Japan

Stylized "truck farm" garden with
native grass and gravel

DEFINING THE CRAFT

HISTORICALLY THE PROFESSION OF LANDSCAPE ARCHITECTURE HAS BEEN DEFINED BY PRACTICE, NOT BY THEORY. FROM VIGNOLA TO LE NÔTRE TO OLMSTED TO CHURCH AND KILEY, THE FINISHED WORK *WAS* THE FIELD. TODAY WE CAN, OF COURSE, ARGUE ABOUT THE BEST WAY TO PRACTICE, BUT FINALLY THE PROFESSION IS A COMPOSITE OF ITS LEADING PRACTITIONERS: THEIR BUILT AND PLANNED WORK, THEIR ORGANIZATIONS AND PROCEDURES, AND THEIR TRAINING METHODS. PETER WALKER AND PARTNERS IS A LANDSCAPE ARCHITECTURE FIRM WITH SIX PARTNERS AND NINE ASSOCIATES, LOCATED IN BERKELEY, CALIFORNIA, AND WORKING WORLDWIDE. ITS WORK RANGES FROM PLANNING TO DETAILED DESIGN, AND IT CARRIES MOST OF ITS DOMESTIC PROJECTS THROUGH

CONSTRUCTION DOCUMENTS AND FIELD SUPERVISION. THE PHOTOGRAPHS IN THIS BOOK RECORD THE FIRM'S BEAUTIFUL AND APPROPRIATE CREATIONS, AND NUMEROUS PROFESSIONAL AWARDS FURTHER ATTEST TO THE EXCELLENCE OF ITS WORK. INDEED, PWP IS ONE OF THE LEADING PRACTITIONERS OF LANDSCAPE ARCHITECTURE IN THE WORLD. THAT MUCH IS EASY TO STATE. WHAT'S DIFFICULT TO EXPLAIN IS THE DISTINGUISHING QUALITY OF THAT EXCELLENCE RELATIVE TO THE SCORES OF OTHER FIRMS CURRENTLY IN PRACTICE AROUND THE WORLD, MANY OF WHICH ARE EXCELLENT IN THEIR OWN RIGHT. AT CONFERENCES OF LANDSCAPE PROFESSIONALS, IT QUICKLY BECOMES APPARENT THAT THE DEFINITION OF LANDSCAPE ARCHITECTURE IS PART OF AN ONGOING DISCUSSION. THERE IS NOT much dispute about the general idea: Landscape architects design land for human purposes. But further discussion produces a welter of refinements: Is landscape architecture a profession? a discipline? an academic specialization? an art? a craft? a science? a trade? a vocation? an ecological testing ground? a small business? a corporate culture? a theoretical field? an environmental stewardship? To an outsider these qualifications seem to offer a smorgasbord of possibilities, few of which necessarily exclude the others. And yet it is clear that the choices a firm makes—consciously or unconsciously—determine not just the kind of work that it will produce but the very possibility of achieving excellence.

For PWP, landscape architecture is the pursuit of a design craft and the management of a small consulting business. These underlying definitions shape the firm. Of course the assumptions behind such definitions work together, but for the sake of order let's say that the vision of landscape architecture as a craft determines who works in the office and the nature of that work, while the consideration of landscape architecture as a small consulting business determines how the firm works with clients and manages the resulting projects.

Among the dictionary definitions of "craft," the most relevant are a) "an occupation or trade requiring manual dexterity or artistic skill" and b) "the members of a trade, or a trade association." Taken together, these definitions suggest one major aspect of day-to-day practice at PWP: transmission of a body of craft knowledge by the masters of that craft to the younger members of the occupational group—in a word, apprenticeship.

The components of the craft of landscape architecture are emblematically expressed in PWP's physical office in a former warehouse near the Berkeley waterfront—a white concrete-block building increasingly covered with the green growth of clipped but vigorous ficus vines. Inside, the "front office" occupies a number of spaces to the south of the building, along with conference rooms, kitchen, library, photography studio, slide archive, and storage facilities. To the north, long rows of three-by-thirty-foot wooden tables fill a high-ceilinged fifty-by-one-hundred-foot room painted white and carpeted in green Astroturf. It is an open studio room. No cubicles, no private offices. At the east end of the room sits Doug Findlay, the partner in charge of project management. Near him sits partner Paul Sieron, a project manager. At the west end sits Tony Sinkosky, the partner in charge of construction. Along the west wall are shelves filled with samples of building materials as well as fake geraniums, fake rocks, and a pile of hard hats. In between Findlay and Sinkosky are the desks of some fifteen to twenty young landscape architects, who are usually hard at work on their computers. Those at Findlay's end tend to be focused on management issues. Those at Sinkosky's, on project implementation.

Peter Walker, Michael Oser,
David Walker, and James A. Lord

In between the management and construction areas sit the designers. Peter Walker, the partner in charge of design, has his own desk close to the construction area. David Walker's is nearer the managers. The men are seldom at their desks. They are usually on their feet moving from one end of the room to the other, behavior that suggests the relationship between the various parts of the craft. For PWP, landscape architecture relies on a knowledge of small-business management and landscape construction, but it is above all a design craft, and the art of design figures into every decision of management and construction.

From the south wall, four twenty-by-sixteen-foot partial walls extend into the room, forming open bays. Within each bay, every inch of both sides of these walls is covered with pinups of currently active projects. Here is where everybody working on a particular project clusters, along with some combination of Findlay, Sieron, the Walkers, and Sinkosky. Here is the overlap, the point of synthesis, where the interaction among the partners, associates, and staff takes place—in front of a range of visual representations: plans, sections, photographs of sites and of possible elements, lists, sketches and drawings of possible details in all scales from 1:5,000 to full size. Materials of all sorts lie scattered about: stacks of stone and concrete, jars of gravels, sections of steel and aluminum check plate and dogeared books about plants from every region of the earth. At a certain point, a beautifully constructed—or, more likely, a partially and repeatedly reconstructed—model will appear on one of the large tables near the walls. These models begin as study tools and are refined throughout the design process as the design ideas are more fully realized and developed. Along with the pinup walls, they are convincing indicators that, whatever the function of a project, whatever its program, the craft of landscape architecture at PWP creates, above all, a visual experience of place.

45

To see landscape architecture as a design craft explains the make-up of the people in the room—most of whom are in their thirties with backgrounds or strong interests in the arts. Many have gone to the Harvard Design School, but there are others from the universities of Illinois, Cal Poly, Pennsylvania, Oregon, Michigan, Berkeley, and the Rhode Island School of Design. After four or five years of undergraduate landscape architecture and/or two or three years of graduate school, students will have learned to use specific computer programs, and they will know something about the history and more about the theory of landscape architecture. But the graduates who want to build actual projects—those who really want to practice—will need to serve an apprenticeship, and they will need to serve it in an office that practices the craft. All except one of the partners at PWP have worked their way up through the firm over the course of twenty years. The exception, Paul Sieron, initially worked for ten years at the firm of William Johnson in Ann Arbor, Michigan.

Doug Findlay and Sarah Kuehl

The apprenticeship can be long—three to five years, maybe more. Some apprentices tend to jump from office to office, the best and the most ambitious looking for mentors who know the craft and are willing to pass it on. Many of the associates at PWP have worked at one time or another for George Hargreaves, Martha Schwartz, or for designers in the SWA Group, who in turn have studied under or worked for or with the principals at PWP. As one associate says, "When I worked for Martha and George, I kept hearing some other 'voice' speaking through their lips. After I began working for Pete, I knew whose voice it was."

The project teams grapple with the day-to-day process of developing an abstract idea to the point at which it can be constructed. Apprentices are quickly integrated into this central action of the firm, and by the time they become associates, they are interacting with the partners and the clients to lead major projects in management, design, or construction, or, increasingly, in all three. A catalogue suggests the scope of their involvement as of this writing: Sarah Kuehl and Doris Schenk are working on the design of the Southwest Federal District of Washington, D.C., and of the Mission Bay campus of the University of California, San Francisco; Paul Buchanan, on construction documentation and observation for the Clark Center at Stanford University, the federal courthouse in Seattle, and the University of California, Merced; James Lord, on the planning and design of Millennium Parklands in Australia and several large projects in New Zealand. Christian Werthmann is working on the final stages of design for the Merced campus of the University of California, while finishing the Clark Center and the Center for Clinical Science Research at Stanford University. Schenk and Liz Einwiller are doing field construction for Barnsdall Park in Los Angeles and Jamison Square in Portland, Oregon. Adam Greenspan is working on the design of the Kramlich residence in Napa and the Glenstone residence outside Washington, D.C., and on the planting plan for the garden of the Nasher Foundation Sculpture Center. Jim Grimes works on construction documents for nearly everything. And Sandy Harris, who has been at PWP for eleven years, continues to work on office administration while providing a communications interface among staff members.

For the apprentice, then, PWP continues to be an ideal educational situation for many years. The work is challenging, and while the associates rely to a great degree on their own considerable skills, there is a vast pool of additional resources, including the partners, who guide them away from major mistakes. Moreover, every young apprentice can look at the example of the associates and know that the principals in the firm want them to succeed, to move up—and to stay. PWP is not intent on using apprentices and then "graduating" them. "We could use more partners and associates this minute," says Findlay.

Tony Sinkosky, Kelly Spokus, and Doris Schenk

Over the course of a year the office will also include a number of interns, some of whom will be invited to return to work full time. There are also professionals from Europe and Asia who come for a year to expand their knowledge. Some stay. There are currently employees from Israel, Germany, Spain, and Switzerland. In recent years, others have come from Japan, South Korea, and the Netherlands. Two of the associates are German and went to German universities: Universitaet Kassel and Technische Universitaet München.

Many apprentices come as generalists who have an interest in everything. Some arrive with a specific interest in management, design, or construction. Almost all see themselves as designers—and as Findlay says, "If you really think about it, there isn't a person out there on that floor who isn't a designer. Whether they're focused on technical, managerial, or contractual issues, they are encouraged to think about it in design terms."

If we were to choose one word to describe the atmosphere of the PWP office, it would be "earnest." The apprentices know that they are working with some of the best in the field, and there is always the driving urgency of the current projects. There is also a poignant sense of the importance of education. Transmitting the craft knowledge guarantees its survival and assures that it will be added to and improved. Peter Walker remembers that in the not-so-distant past an important body of knowledge was lost. He explains: "All landscape architects in the postwar period began, largely, without precedent because the activity of landscape practice in the middle of the twentieth century was interrupted for almost twenty years by the Depression and World War II. Almost all of the traditions of the profession—and, more particularly, the expertise of landscape architecture—were lost with the passing of an older generation."

In addition, the type of projects changed dramatically. Before the Depression "the thrust of the profession was to higher and higher levels of refinement on behalf of the wealthy; during the Depression what was largely estate work was replaced by work for the WPA (Work Projects Administration) and Parks departments. It was much less ambitious and much less artistic, much more democratic and popular." Then, after World War II, Walker explains, "came a new burst of wealth. But it was vested in corporations and in various institutions. The new clients were the universities that grew from ten thousand students to fifty thousand; the cities that went from one hundred thousand to one million, two million; transportation departments with rural roads that became freeways. The new 'estates' were the backyards of the middle-class families who were rushing to the suburbs. Landscape architects had tremendous challenges, but relatively little technique." To face these challenges they not only needed an updated version of the old craft knowledge, they also needed a new kind of office structure that could deal with the new types and scales of work.

Jeff Ulm, Chris Varesi, Janet Beagle, and April Deerr

The great innovator in this regard was Hideo Sasaki, whose story has been told at length in Melanie Simo's *Offices of Hideo Sasaki* (Spacemaker Press, 2001). Sasaki reinvented the landscape architecture office at Sasaki Associates in Watertown, Massachusetts, while serving as chair of Harvard's Department of Landscape Architecture. Walker explains that Sasaki Associates was a combination of two older formats for architectural offices: the corporate firm, "in which you had the internal structuring—a set of collaborating teams—that could take on really large tasks," and the atelier that coalesced around one very senior designer. In the new hybrid office, Sasaki became what Walker describes as "the educational director, the theoretical director, almost the director in an ivory tower." Walker, who was first Sasaki's student, then his employee, next his partner, and finally the head of a new West Coast branch of Sasaki, Walker and Associates, was always more hands-on. Never an ivory-tower type, he managed, he designed, and he constructed—and he has continued to do so for what will soon be fifty years. For PWP one of the advantages of his long tenure (coupled with the twenty-year-long association of Findlay and Sinkosky) is that even though the firm has not built some types of projects for years—the elementary school, say, or the housing development—they still know how to go about it. Unlike the landscape architects after World War II, they have knowledge of a wide range of project types, of their technical challenges, of their planning and context, and of their clients. When new challenges arise, there's something at hand to build on.

On the West Coast Walker quickly acquired a reputation for reinventing himself. After almost twenty years he left what had by then become The SWA Group to be an artist in New York City, came back to the profession as head of the department at Harvard, and reentered practice (now with student Findlay in tow) in a small office that aspired to be more theoretical and more artistic than the corporate firms. PWP is the latest version of that small experimental design firm, which has had a number of names over the years depending on its make-up: SWA East, The Office of Peter Walker and Martha Schwartz, Peter Walker William Johnson and Partners. It has returned to a version of the older office form, the atelier: a group of apprentices clustered around a group of masters. No one, however, is quicker than Walker to acknowledge the debt PWP owes to the larger corporate firms. Sasaki Associates and The SWA Group frequently served as an Early Warning System for PWP: "For the first few years they were always one or two years ahead of us," says Walker, "and we could look at the things they did, in organization and personnel, for example, and decide whether or not we wanted to do them."

Three important lessons from the Early Warning System are now in place at PWP. One is the ESOP, the employee stock ownership plan, modeled on that of The SWA Group. "There's nothing to own in a firm beyond the talent and skill of a group of people, and so the people with the talent and the skills should own the firm," says Walker. "An ESOP builds up the estate of each individual in the firm, and everyone becomes a little more financially secure as time goes by." A second lesson concerns the organization of projects. Both Sasaki Associates and The SWA Group had a designer and a manager paired on every project, as well as some sort of a field group that was a recognizable entity within the firm.

Paul Buchanan and Taya Rhodes

48

Perhaps the most important lesson concerns size. PWP began in San Francisco in the early 1980s, but it really began to grow in 1985, fueled by one project, the Solana campus of IBM, located between Dallas and Fort Worth, Texas. Here the firm was asked to take over the planning and site development of a corporate headquarters on an 850-acre site. "IBM said they would give us all the resources we needed to do it," Walker recalls. "We felt that the office was too small for the job, and we went from six or seven people to fifteen the following year and to twenty the year after that." Findlay was the project manager for Solana, Walker was the project designer, and Sinkosky was in charge of construction and field supervision. "We had aspirations of doing highly refined work, and so, even though we grew, we purposely limited ourselves in two ways," explains Walker. "One, unlike our parent firms, we said we would have no branch offices. We would not use the corporate expansion technique of regional marketing. And, two, we would limit ourselves to around thirty people, which was and is about as many as we can work with closely, face to face, and produce highly refined work." Another important consideration: When a firm has more than thirty employees, it has to focus too heavily on business management.

In the mid-1980s Jane Williamson, now a partner, came in as "someone who could coordinate billing, bookkeeping, the bank, the insurance." She set up the systems and eventually put them on a professional footing—no easy feat. Today she stays on top of the changing world of office management in areas that affect the firm both internally and, ultimately, in its outside projects: computer systems, correspondence, health systems, insurance, foreign employees, liability, government reviews, and security clearances, to name but a few. The professional management of these elements means that young designers can spend their time designing rather than writing memoranda, answering the telephone, and sorting the mail.

Still, business management in the sense of someone's dictating decisions about design on the basis of profit and loss has always been missing from PWP. Findlay explains: "We do not have an umbrella financial basis to our practice, and we never, ever, ever go out into the middle of the room and say, 'We're stopping work because the project is out of money.' We think about it in the same way that an artist accepts and completes a commission. From our first days together our foundation has always been design; all of the other internal and external functions revolve around ideas and the pursuit of our artistic goals and craft." This is particularly important for the way PWP interacts with the apprentices. "If you want inquisitive, energetic, ambitious young people to stay focused on the heart of the project," says Findlay, "you must unhinge the design process from the dominance of a corporate structure based on profit margins." One way PWP makes ends meet, then, is to keep the size of the firm small and attract clients "by focusing on ideas and their careful execution."

Adam Greenspan, Liz Einwiller,
Jim Grimes, and John Bela

Another ambition of the firm is to do planning. PWP is keenly aware, however, that there is much at stake when a landscape architecture office includes physical planning in its practice. Once aspects of the same field, planning split off from landscape architecture in the 1930s, and both have suffered from the divorce—landscape architecture losing the decision-making powers over the larger environment, planning alienated from the design of the land and the physical consequences of decision-making. PWP is trying to bridge the rift. In October 1992, William Johnson joined the office, moving from his Michigan firm, which had been primarily a planning practice. "Bill's coming on board changed the way people within this physically oriented firm looked at things," says Walker. "It was an education, a broadening of our interest." This interest continued after Johnson's retirement in March 1997, and in recent years physical planning—primarily of university and corporate campuses and urban-renewal areas—has accounted for some twenty percent of PWP's projects.

PWP attracts work in a number of ways. The firm takes part in competitions, and it is frequently hired by architects, some of them repeatedly over the years: Helmut Jahn of Murphy/Jahn, Inc.; Yoshio Taniguchi of Taniguchi and Associates; Skidmore, Owings & Merrill; Foster and Partners; Legorreta Arquitectos; Arata Isozaki of Arata Isozaki and Associates; Charles Gwathmey of Gwathmey Siegel; and David Neuman, campus architect at Stanford University. In addition clients come directly to PWP. Many are attracted by the firm's reputation, and one of Walker's main roles has been to speak and write for the firm, to present its public face in competitions, client meetings, and such quasi-ceremonial events as professional conferences and colloquia. He points to the expanded role of the media in acquiring work, especially international projects: "People call us up because they've read or heard something about us."

Most clients hire PWP for a design. "They come for our ideas and our craft. If a prospective client is looking for someone to merely follow a predetermined process and produce a standardized product, they will never hire us," says Findlay. "Clients are attracted to us because they can access decades of experience working at a very high level of landscape architecture design. And we're geared to maximizing the client's resources. If you look at our track record on university campuses, on settings of corporations with very limited funds, you'll see that—compared with other work—what we're producing is far and away more imaginative, inspiring, and recognizable as design on a dollar-for-dollar basis."

Sieron points out that another small, sophisticated group of clients—again, frequently architects—comes to PWP for carefully produced construction documents: "They want a certain level of finish—walls that stand, pavements that drain, plants that live and grow—and they are concerned about how much they invest and the return on that investment. They don't want a lot of unanticipated change orders."

Paul Buchanan and Gilat Lovinger

Although the firm is involved with an amazing diversity of projects at any one time, each project—guided by the design/management team—moves forward more smoothly than a nonlandscape architect would ever expect. The experienced project managers like Findlay and Sieron love what they do because they understand all of the design, construction-document, and field aspects; because they appreciate the political and financial implications; and because they are the sorts of people who *like* to know things. As Sieron admits, "I know about most of the projects in the office. Even if I'm not working on them, I still pretty much know what's going on." Above all, good project managers see the whole process. They are capable of understanding what's essential to a project and then communicating that to others.

Findlay tells how he realized in his second year of graduate school at the Harvard Design School, in a design studio with Walker, that "the activity I was most interested in—which is putting all the parts of a project together—is, frankly, meaningless unless there is an artistic heart to the project, a design idea." Findlay sees the most important parts of management as communicating the design idea and making sure that it lives to see the light of day. "A firm like ours struggles daily to keep the design issues in focus, because this, above all, is our purpose—a design—and a really good idea is an extremely fragile entity. There are so many issues that come up in the course of a project that are much more powerful than the design idea, and if you don't treat it with care and dignity and nurture it and protect it, it will never survive. I consider myself a designer. I just happen to use contracts and telephone calls and faxes and e-mails to map the route that a design idea has to navigate through the maze." To see Findlay at work is to come to appreciate the arts of communication and persuasion.

One of the most important aspects of ushering the design idea through the maze is to understand the desires of the client. "The relationship of a client's desires to the idea at the heart of the project is still to this day the aspect that I enjoy most," says Findlay. This relationship requires a lot of work. For one thing, the client needs to get excited about the project. "To convince a client, who has never envisioned the idea, to invest money, time, and energy in it, to take the risk that's required to build artful landscapes that ultimately inspire people, that's pretty cool. You're producing something that has value, that exposes people to something they've never seen before, that changes their perspectives. If you've achieved a level of excitement in clients of the caliber we work with, then you've gone a long way toward building something with lasting value."

Frequently the job of the designer/manager is one of translation. "A lot of people have a fundamental human interest in landscape and they've already formed their opinions. While opinions about architecture aren't so precisely formed, we all seem to be born with a landscape notion in our minds. Clients have very strong opinions about the feeling that the landscape project should produce," says Findlay. "Words like 'formal' and 'informal,' 'straight' and 'curved,' words like 'natural' come up all the time. It would be fascinating to invite all our past and current clients to debate their different definitions of those words. So that's where the translation comes in. You must tune into the client wavelength and understand what landscape means to them."

51

David Walker, Conny Roppel,
Nadine Dreyer, Moritz Moellers,
Matthias Wehrle, Paul Sieron, and
Janet Beagle

Compromise in this process is not only possible, it's rewarding. "In successful projects the basic idea is realized," Findlay says, "but in every project you can see how most pieces have morphed into a slightly different configuration in reaction to a discovery or a constraint. Often the essence of an idea has had to become clearer and more powerful just to survive." The everyday back-and-forth of working with a project team strengthens the design because it forces a careful examination of the idea. Projects aren't very successful when there "isn't enough testing of the idea, of how it works and what it really produces. Projects that haven't been challenged typically don't have a lot of richness or depth to them."

The perilous state of the design idea continues throughout the process of getting the project built. "Obstacles during construction," says Findlay, "can involve everything from the laws of gravity to regulations. It's a problem when you have a great artistic idea and you think you're going to overpower the laws of the State of California or the ADA requirements." And unforeseen events always occur. "When an idea enters the construction arena, it's just as fragile as it was on the first day," says Findlay. "We often catch ourselves thinking that once we've got it drawn, all the problems are solved. Well, it's not true."

The challenges of bringing the project through to the end have increased over time, according to Walker: "In the 1960s we just needed to move fast and get it done, and nobody paid an awful lot of attention. Today, we work through an excruciating bureaucratic and financial system that is always reviewing, looking for flaws, looking for failures, looking for higher levels of performance." Since this system increases the time it takes to finish projects and, hence, the amount of money involved, clients learn to value firms that know how to negotiate the maze.

Much of this negotiation involves knowing when to give in and when to stand firm. As one associate says, "One thing I've learned from this office is when to say 'yes' and when to say 'no.' If you have a strong design and you know it's a strong design, you can have the whole world beating down your back saying, 'No, no, no, it's not going to work,' and you can stand your ground. But you also need to know when to listen. You need to know when to convince and when to be convinced."

Although the garden has been defined in any number of ways, one notion common to most definitions is that the garden brings humans into relationship with nature. It would perhaps be more accurate to say that the garden brings humans into relationship with their own *ideas* about nature, for it was only when man perceived himself as a creature apart from nature—a moment in intellectual history—that he felt the need to put himself into relationship with something that was, until that defining moment, simply the environment of his being. As a further development, we might wonder if the modern garden came into being at the time when we humans began to question the external reality of our metaphysical systems, when we began to understand how, as symbol-making animals, we busily spend every moment inventing our own gods. When we began to suspect that the nature we bring into the garden is one of those divinities—yet another metaphor of our own making—nature becomes a complicated notion indeed: hypernature, as it were, the symbol of a concept.

Sandy Harris and Jane Williamson

All this is to say that in order to succeed at their art, modern garden designers have to bring nature into the garden in a manner that makes it perceivable to human beings at a sophisticated level of understanding. Yet they frequently work in settings where both sides of the perceptual equation are wanting: Sometimes nature is in short supply, and sometimes it has become invisible to the distracted human eye. A tree may carry with it some 15,000 years of human associations, so that every tree has tremendous symbolic potential, but sometimes the existence of the tree is problematic, and sometimes our memories are vague, our imaginations deadened. In the face of these deficiencies, modern garden designers are frequently in the position of supplying nature from extremely limited resources and then making it significant to people who are doing something else—running to catch a train, working, jogging, flirting, eating lunch.

The ability to make nature visible—and meaningful—in difficult situations is one aspect of PWP's excellence as landscape architects that has not been sufficiently appreciated, perhaps because the difficulty is frequently disguised by success. PWP's design strategies are, nevertheless, as much characterized by the difficult nature of the project sites as by any recognizable stylistic mannerisms. The projects that have the greenest, most "naturalistic" look to them—the new University of California campus at Merced, for example—are frequently located on sites that have, at worst, been used for agricultural purposes. Sites like this are rare. Other sites are simply degraded and must be regenerated: the Toyota Municipal Museum of Art in Japan, for example, or the McConnell Foundation in Redding, California. In both of these projects, the design exploits the required restoration of the natural setting. The replanted forest at Toyota frames the cultural institutions, setting into contrast the "designed" planting around the museum. At McConnell the refined hardscape near the building directs the human gaze out to the regenerated ponds, meadows, and hills.

53

The sites of a great many other PWP projects have been so heavily used that they are essentially devastated and, as far as nature goes, virtually a clean slate, the much-maligned tabula rasa: for example, the center of Nishi Harima Science Garden City in Japan, destroyed by previous construction, or the Sony Center in Berlin, a site that has been urban for so long that even the memory of its indigenous nature—a marshy swamp—has evaporated. And then, increasingly, there are those projects that really have no natural site at all because they are built over structure: the Hotel Kempinski in Munich, for example, or, most evocatively, Saitama Plaza in Japan, where a re-created natural drainage system has been lifted eight meters above the ground.

PWP frequently reestablishes a human perception of nature through the artistic manipulation of the patterns, forms, and elements that have become familiar to man from millennia of garden design and, before that, agricultural use: the row, the orchard, the pond, the paved farm courtyard, the bosque, the allée, the wall, the bench. We think of the tree-lined canals at the University of California at Merced; the larch grove and the irises at the Toyota Municipal Museum; the 220 zelkova trees at Saitama Plaza, which are conceptually related to the zelkova allée and mixed grove at the Hikawa Shrine a mile or so away. We also think of the fake—not faux—rocks at Nishi Harima and the cantilevered pool at the Sony Center, which reminds us that nature now exists on a structure that extends above, below, and behind us—in historical as well as physical terms.

*Daphne Edwards, Moritz Moellers,
and Gabriel Meil*

As an inspiration for his work Walker has frequently cited the Minimalists of the 1960s and 1970s as well as the seventeenth-century French designer Andre Le Nôtre—especially such gardens as Chantilly and Courances in which the style is reduced to its basic geometries. In PWP's recent work we can see the influence of Minimalism. A few elemental moves are presented visually and with elegance. The projects are nonrepresentational—neither narrative nor symbolic in any straightforward way—but "the thing itself" made highly visible: Even the fake rocks are really fake rocks that light up the night and proclaim their true nature. Particularly in photographs some projects like Library Walk at University of California at San Diego have the directness and strength of Minimalist installations. We can contemplate those photographs in a metaphysical frame of mind. But when we see Library Walk at noon swarming with students, all busy with their own thoughts, it may strike us that the issue of function changes everything. Perhaps a craft takes inspiration from its own history because of the special factors that pertain only to that craft? Noontime at Versailles at the height of the tourist season suggests that the craft of garden design is far more influential in the work of PWP than fine art, even Minimalism. The ability to absorb program—often including vast numbers of people—while maintaining an air of mystery and at least the possibility of significance is part of the craft of garden design that PWP espouses. As Donald Judd once warned, "The designer eliminates function at his peril." One idea of the Minimalists has had an overwhelming impact on PWP's work: the realization that if only a few things are being "made visible" at any one time, then those things must be not only capable of attracting attention, but also worth being seen. Much of the energy of the office, and especially that of the younger designers, is directed to attaining this level of refinement. This is *the* reason that many of them have come. As Jane Williamson puts it with characteristic understatement, "PWP has a reputation for rather high standards."

The reactions of various associates to working with Walker tell a lot about the design process at PWP. One associate says, "As a junior-designer kind of person you have a lot of influence in the intermediate scale. You really find the stones and decide how big they are. You make a lot of decisions that are in between what Pete does and what Tony does that actually shape the product. And if you really believe in design at that scale, there's a ton to be learned and it's stuff that you don't learn in school." Another puts it in a different light: "I have argued with Pete over an eighth of an inch. It's amazing that we can have a broad concept that ties together two acres, and it still all gets down to whether it's an eighth-inch joint or a quarter-inch joint."

What is finally important is how those details contribute to the whole scheme. Another associate explains: "It's a kind of mediation. Pete tries to explain to you what he wants, and then you come up with something. You think about all the small details. Pete comes in, without knowing all the small details. It's an advantage. He sees the big picture and doesn't get lost in all the small stuff, and he says, 'Hey, what are you guys doing here? This won't work!' It's a judgment call based on his experience of the big picture. So he explains, and you do another round. You have to hold yourself back and try to feel the lead designer's intent, and this is probably the hardest lesson for anyone who comes straight from school into an office with a strong designer."

Taya Rhodes, Kelly Spokus, and Susan Pinto

54

Difficult or not, the office is the best place for apprentices to learn to design. Here it is real. The lessons have actual repercussions in built work. At PWP practice is the operative theory. In accord with Minimalist belief, practice is "the thing itself": landscape architecture as a profession. And for the partners, and increasingly for the associates, the office is the best place to teach. No matter how highly ranked a design school is, teachers will never have a class of students who are this good, who bring so much energy and enthusiasm to the actual building of real projects.

The shortest explanation of PWP's concern with construction is that the office is trying to do work at a high level of refinement in a modern, technical, risk-averse, highly litigious society. No short explanation can, however, convey the amount of energy and intelligence that goes into this pursuit. There is an intense interest in choosing each material, deciding on its technical use, and then finding its source. Today PWP literally searches the world for the materials that go into its landscapes. Materials are, however, only part of the story; what's done with them counts for even more. PWP regularly does more grading than most firms do—and with a great deal more care. Benches, bollards, tree grates, walls, steps, pavements, pools, fountains, and planting must never draw attention by sloppy workmanship.

Listening to the younger landscape architects in the office, even if only briefly, brings home the intensity of this concern. With the associates who work with Tony Sinkosky in construction and field supervision, the conversation, not surprisingly, quickly moves to materials. At PWP it sometimes seems as if the metaphorical statement of "no stone going unturned" has been transformed into literal truth. We are told about the long pavers—three by twenty-four inches long—in a courtyard between the two buildings at the Center for Clinical Sciences at Stanford University. The courtyard had to be perfectly flat but also drain. The custom-made concrete pavers were set in sand, and underneath the sand bed is a permeable concrete that, as Sinkosky says, "is challenging to pour because if you compact it too much it won't be porous. There's only one supplier and the contractor was scared of it. But we finally got it done, and so far water is going through."

And then there are the pavers in the entrance courtyard at the McConnell Foundation, made of a very hard form of granite and laid on their sides in sand to create a paving four inches thick. Had the pavers been laid in mortar, they would have been prohibitively expensive, but using a low-tech method and a leftover material made the sophisticated paving of the courtyard affordable—and, hence, possible.

There's also a lot of discussion about the cobblestones at the Clark Center at Stanford University. As one associate says, "We wanted them laid in a random pattern—no rectangular pattern, no continuous joints, irregular. Only a very few masons can still do that. It's very complicated, like putting a puzzle together. Tony found that American contractors couldn't do it. So he developed a module, a twenty-four-square-inch module with three different sizes of stones pieced together so that they look random." Associate after associate suggests what one finally says outright: "Tony is so proficient and inventive and he has such a vast library in his brain that he can solve a problem in any number of different ways."

Gisela Steber, Tim Wight, and Annette Flores

Beyond the turning of stones lies a fierce determination to make these landscapes last, so that the care in construction is not only a matter of aesthetics. It's also a matter of function and, therefore, concern with plant selection, plant health, chemical and mechanical composition of soils, long-term maintenance, and safety. To the outsider and even to certain clients, this persistent inventiveness and obsessive care sometimes seem almost religious, more driven than purely practical. But again there is, at least in part, a historical explanation. After the twenty years of the Depression and World War II, at the time of the great burgeoning of large-scale projects in the United States, much of the lore of landscape construction had evaporated. Moreover, civil engineers had disappeared from the offices of landscape architects. (Sasaki Associates was one of the few firms that managed to bring engineers back in-house while The SWA Group had them for only four years.) Still, a belief in technical proficiency in everything from grading to handrails continued to drive thoughtful work. As for grading, the advent of technology in the form of bulldozers permitted the moving of vast amounts of material. For the landscape this posed a great danger because grading artfully and with respect for the site and its soil composition had not been adequately developed—especially by the engineers who were doing it. Over the past thirty years much of this technical craft has had to be reinvented or learned from other sources, including foreign work, and this may account for some of the intensity that drives PWP's approach.

Another of today's problems is that the detail skills of contractors cannot be taken for granted. Sinkosky sees the solution to this problem in improved communication. "Our younger people come back to me and say, 'The contractor should have known.' And I say, 'Well, guess what? You have to assume he's not going to read your mind.' I say, 'When he looks at this drawing, the information has to jump off the sheet and be absolutely clear.'" Sinkosky is also completely hands-on. "I don't really separate construction documents from construction observations," he says. "Ideally the same people prepare the documents and then watch the construction. You have to know the documents very well in order to communicate and defend the idea. Excellence is not a casual endeavor. It's a full-time, painful process. It's hard work. A lot of people are attracted to the idea of construction and field, but when they find out what it entails, they become less attracted to it." Of course there are others who grow even more interested when they discover the complexities and difficulties, and, not surprisingly, PWP has attracted and repeatedly uses half a dozen consultants who are also drawn by the challenges of excellence—specialists in pavements, drainage, plant materials, fountain and irrigation hydrology, maintenance, and sculpture.

David Walker has a slightly different focus on the firm's current work. After working at PWP for seven years, from the time of Solana to the first projects in Japan, he left to go to graduate school at Harvard, then returned. Today much of the work he does is on foreign projects—especially those with Helmut Jahn as architect. He is also currently working on a research campus for Novartis in Switzerland and on a group of projects with a New Zealand family-held development firm. His tasks include communicating with

56

Peter Walker, Adam Greenspan, and Kari Boeskov

the clients and architects and integrating overseas design and construction. In foreign projects, as opposed to the domestic, local firms are hired to do the detailed construction documents and supervision with PWP oversight. Difficulties are magnified because over the years many European firms have delegated construction drawings and supervision to public agencies. Therefore, PWP has had to find mature, like-minded craftsmen in local landscape offices. "PWP's role is not to call out every nut and bolt in these projects," David Walker explains, "but to define how the project is going to look and then develop relationships with landscape architects who know the local culture, the local building and plant materials, the local regulations. We use local partners the way we work in-house with Tony and the construction department." One of his goals is to develop a group of apprentices within the office who are proficient in this different way of working, one that frequently requires more communications and political skill than technical horsepower.

In some ways the greatest technological advance in the history of the craft of landscape architecture has taken place in recent memory. As one associate puts it, "A huge amount of what we do is act as translators between the older partners and the digital world." The apprentices rely on their computer skills and their general ease with technology, while the partners—with the notable exception of David Walker—rely on manual drawing skills. As the youngest partner, David Walker introduced the firm to the digital revolution; he was the first designer at PWP to use computer technology, beginning with the designs of Sony and Saitama. It can be argued that design at PWP benefits from this interaction of old and new. Drawing by hand is still useful for the initial capture of ideas, and it is arguably necessary for achieving proper scale. But for sheer speed, computers and the related communication technology undoubtedly increase the firm's efficiency, enabling it to work collaboratively and internationally. Video-conferencing, the twenty-four-hour camera directed at the site, and the posting of plans on websites are benefits that come immediately to mind. And yet the political skills of the partners are still necessary—and necessary in the way they are practiced: in face-to-face conferences, telephone conversations, and site visits.

Although the issues and problems facing modern landscape architecture are diverse and may seem daunting, particularly when solutions are intended to be artful, over the course of twenty years a relatively small and ever-evolving studio of dedicated teachers and apprentices has produced a significant body of work that has enlarged the consciousness of the profession and helped define the practice of modern landscape architecture. In the following pages we will look at some of the products of that practice. While it is unfortunately true that photography is not the ideal medium for conveying the truth about anything, particularly landscape, PWP's emphasis on the visual dimension of design assures that the photographic images of their landscapes are closer to truth than is usually the case. All that's missing—alas!—is the smell, the feel, the dimensional experience of reality. And yet, what does any representation do but ask us to consider a less than perfect version of reality?
—*Jane Brown Gillette*

Carmen Arroyo, Jeff Ulm, and Kazu Kobayashi

RECENTLY COMPLETED PROJECTS

IF ARCHITECTURAL DESIGN IS CONSCIOUS BUILDING, THEN COMPLETED PROJECTS ARE THE CLINICAL TESTS OF THE PLANNING AND DESIGN HYPOTHESES, CONCEPTS, AND IDEAS EMERGING FROM THAT CONSCIOUSNESS. THEIR ACHIEVED REALITY TESTS FUNCTIONAL AND AESTHETIC ASSUMPTIONS AS WELL AS SCALE, CRAFT, AND FINALLY USEFULNESS. FAILURES TEACH IMPORTANT LESSONS, WHILE SUCCESS EXPANDS OUR OPPORTUNITIES AND ENCOURAGES A FURTHER REACH. THE FOLLOWING PROJECTS ARE PART OF THIS ONGOING INVESTIGATION.

McConnell Foundation
Redding, California

Redding lies at the north end of California's Sacramento Valley, surrounded on three sides by a magnificent backdrop of mountains. In 1964 Carl R. and Leah F. McConnell established the McConnell Foundation to fund such public projects in the Redding area as new fire engines and equipment, botanical gardens, pedestrian trails, and bridges. By the early 1990s, the endowment had risen in value to hundreds of millions of dollars, and the foundation needed larger administrative quarters that would also increase public awareness of its institutional presence in the community.

The location chosen for the new foundation complex was an ecologically degraded 150-acre suburban site that had been owned for years by a local road contractor, who had created four large ponds by means of roughly graded earthen dams. The site had also been heavily grazed by herds of mules, which had eaten the native shrubs and grasses down to the roots, destroying the grassland ecology and causing serious erosion. All riparian growth had been degraded, and the native tree cover had been reduced to a scattering of live oaks. Furthermore, suburban expansion had brought subdivision housing so close that it could be seen from most areas within the site.

The program called for an executive office and conference center, a separate residence for donors and guests, and a park that would be open to pedestrian visitors, Redding citizens, and, from time to time, large invited groups arriving by car. The park was also to be a demonstration of the ecological repair of a large foothill site.

Neither the site's urbanizing edges nor its existing flora provided inspiration for the siting of the building or the landscape development, but the proximate point of the three largest ponds seemed to be the most dramatic place in the existing landscape— even though the ponds were at quite different levels. The main building, by NBBJ Architects, was placed at the grade of and directly adjacent to the uppermost pond. Architecturally it responds to the angular geometry of the two major earthen dams, which—after partial reconstruction and resurfacing—serve both as functional dams and as angular linear pathways gesturing out from the headquarters to engage the larger site. The building enjoys a panoramic view that includes the lower pond. The middle pond can be viewed from the outdoor entertainment area and from the olive-lined path along the second dam that leads to the guest house. A large lawn rolls down from the upper level to the middle and lower ponds.

A gently winding entrance road, fitted carefully to the existing grade, curves its way through the park. It opens views of the upper pond through an existing stand of oaks and, as it climbs the hill, a large new persimmon grove laid out to accommodate overflow parking. The entry road leads visitors to the generous arrival plaza and parking, which was made less visible by grading the car spaces back into the hillside. The stone-paved arrival plaza is large enough to allow bus turnaround and short-term parking, but its apparent size is scaled down and softened by the shadow pattern of a newly planted cluster of live oaks.

The view from the arrival plaza encompasses a rock "beach" at the edge of the upper pond and a stone jetty that reaches out into the pond, then disappears into a fountain of mist. From the plaza, a long covered walk along the main wing of the headquarters flanks the upper pond. The walk is edged on the pond side with U-shaped benches. A row of stepping stones, which begins on the west lawn and passes through the building, stretches out onto the surface of the upper pond.

At the south end of the major wing is a small island, designed as a memorial to the founders. A seat-high stone wall surrounds a fountain composed of alternating rings of polished black granite and still water that reflect the sky in slightly different ways. A ring of bald cypress borders the island. An uncommon tree in Redding, the bald cypress is a deciduous conifer with a memorable seasonal cycle and, in its native ecology, an association with still water. A garden of exotic grasses separates the path and lawn areas adjacent to the building from the memorial island.

A stone parapet and gravel path parallel the upper dam, creating a linear pedestrian way with a view over the lower pond. A single row of tulip trees reinforces the axis of the path and the wall, which extends into the landscape at the south end of the main building. In the courtyards and the spaces generated by the joining of the wings, fountains and exotic plantings create gardens with different characters for each of the offices within.

The whole park has been regraded to the smooth forms of its previous foothill contours. Topsoil has been replaced and sowed with native flowering grasses. All riparian areas have been reestablished, extending the green of the grassland landscape in the spring and providing a strong contrast to the yellow, then yellow-gray of the surrounding unirrigated meadows in the late summer, fall, and winter. A major reforestation has already been accomplished at the outer limits of the site and in the subdivision that was purchased by the foundation for visual protection.

right
Main dam promenade

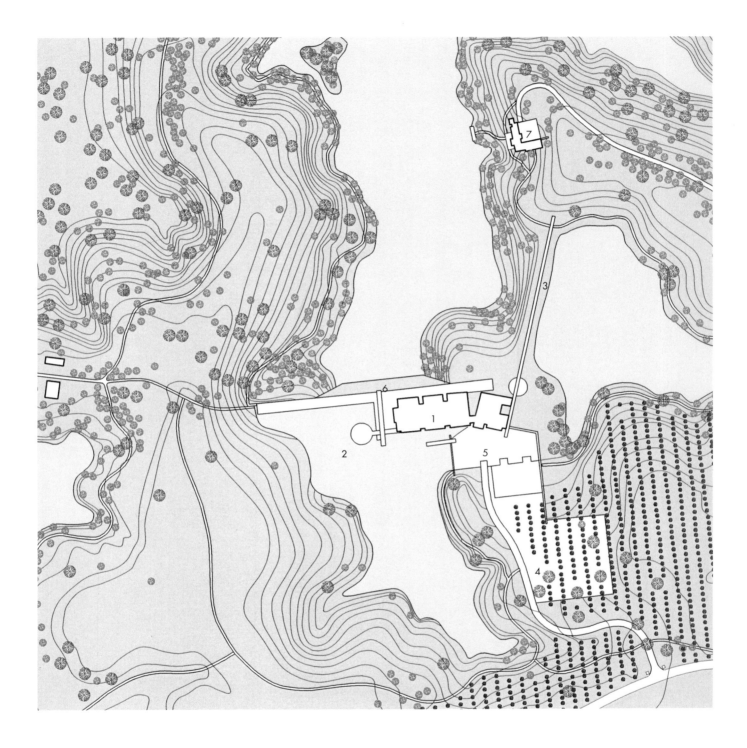

62

Landscape plan

1   McConnell Foundation headquarters
2   Memorial
3   Allée of olive trees
4   Persimmon orchard
5   Entry court
6   Earthen dam with cascade
7   Guest house

top

Screening of adjacent housing

Olive allée

bottom

Main dam reconstruction

Replanting of native grass

64

New riparian planting
on main pond

top	*middle*	*bottom*
Equisetum at memorial bench	*Pier with mist fountain*	*Still fountain at the memorial*
Bubble fountain	*Floating stones*	*Marsh planting*
Stone beach	*Founder's memorial fountain*	*Reeds*

Portland Parks and Jamison Square
Portland, Oregon

In 1999 PWP won a competition to prepare the master plan for a series of parks in Portland's Riverfront District, a new area of housing and offices northwest of downtown and adjacent to the Pearl Arts District. On the master plan three new parks would extend across Naito Parkway and the main rail line to City-owned Centennial Mills, a complex of historic structures on the riverfront, which is to be developed as a continuous recreation, pedestrian, and bicycle way.

Rather than continue the format of the city's famous linear parks, which date back to Olmsted, the proposed parks take the form of a series of individual square blocks, surrounded and separated by housing and retail/commercial buildings. While accepting the idea of individual neighborhood parks, PWP felt that the strong linearity of the sweep from the Pearl Arts District down Tenth Avenue to the riverfront was the basis of a useful design concept: Continuous elements would join the four distinct parks (including one at the riverfront), each with its own image but together forming a gestural whole.

The continuous elements would consist of a pedestrian boardwalk running along the Tenth Avenue edge of each park and its adjacent development blocks, then rising over the highway and tracks to connect to the river. Along the developed blocks, retail

shops would be required to front on the boardwalk. Two other elements would link the parks. First, a gallery of decomposed granite and orcharded hornbeam trees would establish a series of spaces for outdoor art shows and festivals. These galleries would fill the quarter of each park adjacent to the boardwalk. Lights and park furniture would continue through the three neighborhood parks. Second, adjacent to the outdoor gallery, each park would, in different ways, metaphorically express the idea of an "aquifer" supplying water to the rest of the park.

For Jamison Square, the first completed park, the master plan and alternative park designs were reviewed and discussed in well-attended neighborhood workshops and then further developed under review of the City agencies and boards concerned with parks, forestry, transportation, and urban design.

A complex stepped stone wall (the metaphorical expression of an aquifer) divides the gallery from the balance of the park. Water cascades from the many levels of the stone wall, then spreads out to fill a shallow semicircular basin. At its fullest, the water recedes, disappearing back into the base of the wall, then playfully flows out again. The wall offers many levels for climbing and sitting, each level with a slightly different relationship to the cascade, which soaks some

and leaves others dry. The water flow is always gentle and shallow enough for toddlers to enjoy. When the fountain is turned on, the paved plaza becomes a beach. Beyond the beach, a semicircle of grass provides space for more relaxed—and drier—play. When the fountain is turned off, the basin becomes a shallow amphitheater.

Planting in the grass and plaza consists of deodar cedar and Himalayan birch; a hornbeam grove forms the gallery; and a double row of honey locust lightly shades the comfortable wooden-backed benches along the boardwalk. At the west edge, three colorful totems by Kenny Scharf, commissioned by the Pearl Arts Foundation, overlook the fountain and park.

In the summer the park draws hundreds of users from the entire city. If Lovejoy Fountain is for apartment and condominium residents and Forecourt Fountain for teenagers and young adults, then Jamison Square speaks to young children accompanied by their parents and grandparents.

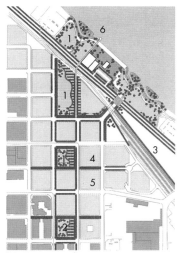

1 Parks
2 Jamison Square
3 "Aquifer"
4 Boardwalk
5 Outdoor gallery
6 Willamette River

Landscape plan for Jamison Square

1 Lawn
2 Pond and amphitheater
3 "Aquifer" stone fountain wall
4 Boardwalk
5 Outdoor gallery

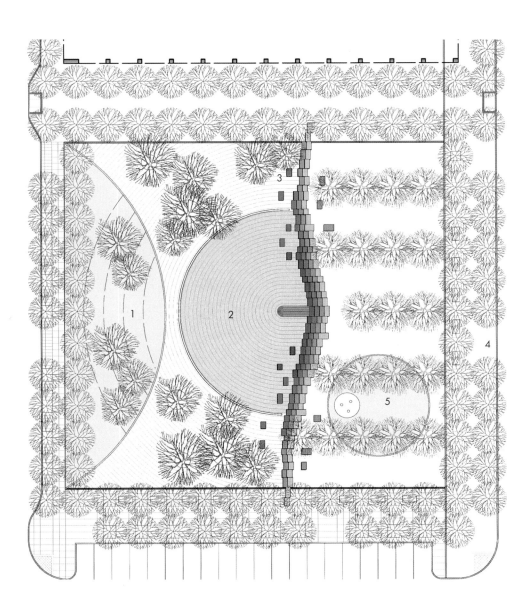

Wave fountain

69

Park in the summer

Civic Park at Martin Luther King Jr.
Promenade
San Diego, California

Civic Park and San Diego

In 1987 PWP won an invited competition to plan a new linear park along San Diego's old Embarcadero. The result was Marina Linear Park now renamed Martin Luther King Jr. Promenade. The plan for the linear park was to be implemented over the years in sections, as developers installed the portion connected to their frontage.

The extended promenade emphasizes the linear movement of trains, cars, light rail, bicycles, and joggers. Bench seating and viewing areas are recessed into the triangular spaces formed when the axis of the promenade meets the grid of the city streets. The constant, complex linear movement recalls the activity of the former Embarcadero.

In 1995, in preparation for the Republican National Convention, the San Diego Redevelopment Agency commissioned PWP to design the centerpiece of the promenade opposite the twin convention hotels at the foot of First and Front streets. The park had to accommodate the Santa Fe Railroad and the light rail, which cross the west side of the site.

The master plan for Civic Park called for a large circular reflecting pool that would resolve the conflicting geometry of the Embarcadero and the grid of the city to the north. PWP's solution uses a rustic stone wall in an interrupted form to create a rotated square joining the pool to a park that picks up the city grid. The pool is backed by a series of circular grass mounds formed in partial spheres. An irregular planting of pine, scattered within a system of decomposed-granite paths, throws shadows on the paths at noon, while the strong San Diego sun makes the green spheres intensely visible within the shadowed grove. The seat-high stone wall penetrates several of the grass spheres as it passes through the park.

An allée of Italian cypress lines the sidewalk on First and Front streets, reinforced by bright magenta "buttons" of iceplant.

Section of grass mounds with pine

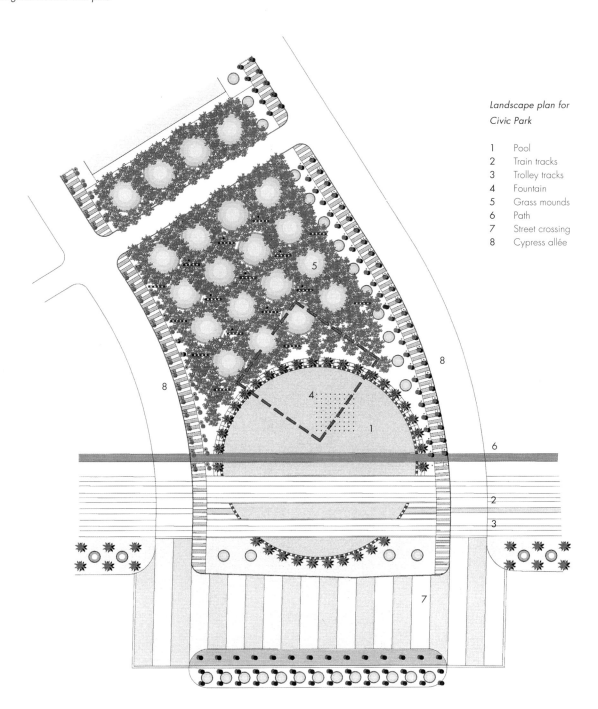

Landscape plan for
Civic Park

1   Pool
2   Train tracks
3   Trolley tracks
4   Fountain
5   Grass mounds
6   Path
7   Street crossing
8   Cypress allée

left

Grass mounds and pine

top

Civic Park

bottom

Stone bench

Path through the park

74

top
Kinetic rain fountain
Palms and iceplant buttons

bottom
Road and railroad through
the park
Curved cypress allée

right
Play pool with rain fountain

Bayer Headquarters
Leverkusen, Germany

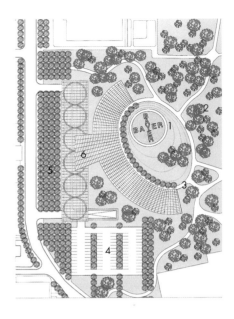

A new headquarters/meeting building is the first of a series of projects that will modernize and expand the administrative offices of Bayer A.G., the pharmaceutical giant. The site is located on the edge of a 100-acre nineteenth-century English-style park that for years has served as the open-space center of the Bayer complex. The new semicircular headquarters building, designed by Murphy/Jahn, Inc., is adjacent to a company-operated restaurant and hotel housed in a nineteenth-century building that opens out onto a terrace overlooking the park.

Each of the company buildings facing Kaiser Wilhelm Allée has an automobile entry or porte-cochere, as does the new headquarters building. A bosque of clipped sycamore trees with benches serves as both a formal entry to the new building and a pedestrian pathway connecting the automobile entry to the sidewalk and the adjacent restaurant and hotel building. The new headquarters, which is completely glass, looks out, northwards, over the sycamore bosque to existing research and administration buildings and, southwards, over a curved arcade of pollarded sycamore trees to the green, tree-edged meadows of the park. The traditional gently curving paths of the park join the curved arcade path to fit the modern building seamlessly into the larger landscape. A circular reflecting pool is set into a sunken oval of lawn between the curved arcade and the park.

The reflecting pool repeats the famous Bayer logo, which appears throughout the larger complex. In certain lights the pool reflects the building, making the logo almost invisible. In others, it becomes more apparent. At night, the pool reflects the building while lighting within the pool subtly emphasizes the logo. Together, bosque, building, and pool provide a distinctly modern event that is, nevertheless, fully integrated with the traditional European surroundings.

Landscape plan

1   Bayer pool
2   Nineteenth-century park
3   Lawn
4   Parking
5   Bosque
6   Porte-cochere

right
Bayer pool and park beyond
Path at building
Bayer pool

Saitama Plaza
Saitama, Japan

An open competition was held in 1994 for the design of a plaza that would serve as the pedestrian core of a newly planned subcenter of greater Tokyo. Built over a huge existing rail yard, the center was intended to relieve access congestion to the older district centers of the city and would include a new train station, the largest arena in Tokyo, the tallest building in Japan, and millions of square meters of new office, residential, and retail space.

The competition attracted hundreds of submissions from Japan and overseas, almost all of them postmodern, historicist, or deconstructive in style, with wild circular and diagonal gestural elements above and below the second level of the plaza.

OHTORI Consultants put together a team with NTT UD Architects and asked PWP to lead in the design. The team took an approach far different from the other competitors, metaphorically borrowing a square of the forest surrounding the nearby Hikawa Shrine and placing this calm natural element in a perfectly classical grid at the center of the gigantic new urban construction. The plaza was conceived as a fifth "elevation" of an otherwise totally glass building containing a shopping center at ground level. Each tree on the plaza apparently rises from a steel pillar in the floor below.

The most unusual aspect of the plaza is its absolute flatness—a concept that was an extension of previous work on the Marlborough Roof Garden (1979), the Cambridge Roof Garden (1979), and Sony Center (1992). A paving of cast-aluminum grills and narrow strips of stone emphasizes this flatness. Beneath the surface lie 1.5 meters of specially designed soil in which 220 matched zelkova trees are planted in specially designed structural supports. A deciduous tree with a vase-shaped structure, the zelkova is one of Japan's most popular trees. At each point of vehicular access the soil is "revealed" by panels in the spandrel—an effect reminiscent of Walter de Maria's *New York Earth Room.* Rainwater moves first through the flat grillage of the plaza surface, then down through the earth layer, where it is finally collected and drained. The construction detailing and installation supervision by the landscape architects of OHTORI Consultants and NTT UD Architects are at the very highest level of craft.

Rising up from the street level, through the plaza and the tree canopy, are four glass towers containing stairs, elevators, and restaurant and café service at street, plaza, tree-canopy, and above-canopy levels. Grand stairs are placed at each of the open sides of the plaza with additional elevators and escalators between the shopping and plaza levels. Plaza-level connections to adjacent buildings and the train station facilitate the pedestrian movement of huge crowds. The plaza also includes a small police kiosk; a lighted piazza for music and dance, which becomes an ice-skating rink in winter; café chairs; a small grass area for children's play; and a system of wooden benches with set-in panels for cultural announcements. Lighting for the plaza comes from the wooden benches, from the glass piazza, from the glass towers, and from beneath the grillage.

Wooded shrine and allée

Wooded Hikawa Shrine

Concept diagram

Model showing raised earth layer at stair

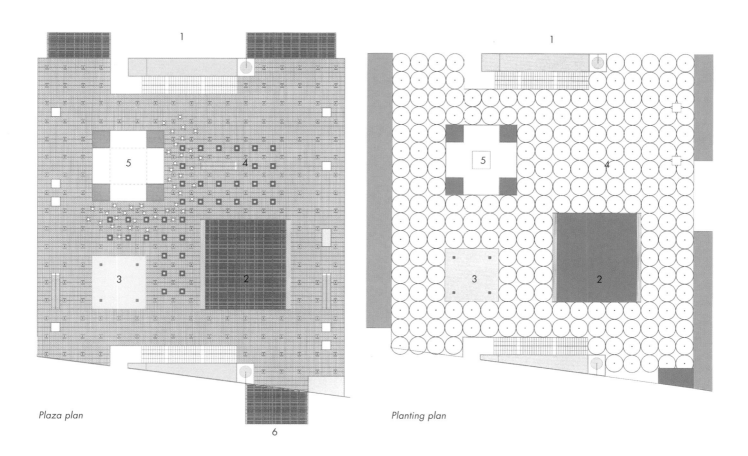

Plaza plan

Planting plan

Landscape plans

1 Stairway
2 Plaza and skating rink
3 Lawn
4 Zelkova orchard
5 Glass tower
6 Bridge

pages 80-81
Festival plaza and skating rink
with lights beneath

pages 82-85
Zelkova grove

Aerial view of forest and dining
tower in spring

top
Earth layer and great stair
Forest in fall color

bottom
Inner court of tower
Lighting from beneath paving grill

Sony Center
Berlin, Germany

Sony Center in Berlin is the result of three staged competitions held over several years. The program included a series of mid-rise office and apartment blocks, Sony's European headquarters, a rebuilt historic hotel, a film house and museum, a Cineplex, an IMAX theater, and a public plaza surrounded by cafés and restaurants. Comprising approximately one third of the reconstructed Potsdamer Platz—the traditional gateway to Berlin from the east—the complex expresses Sony's intent to extend its market to the newly independent nations of Eastern Europe.

The major feature of the landscape is the great plaza, more than 360 feet in length, surrounded by buildings and partially covered by Helmut Jahn's immense "tent," rising seven stories above the street level. The interior of the plaza, rather than the frontage on the outside street, is lined with cafés and shops. The tent and the lining of buildings modify temperature extremes by as much as ten degrees, thus extending comfortable use of the plaza throughout much of the year. The plaza is mostly open and, therefore, available to such planned events as art,

boat, and car shows as well as various performances, yet it conveys a festival atmosphere even when it is not activated by a specific program or event. The plaza, which is nearly flat, is paved with alternating bands of cast-steel grates and the traditional black granite cobbles that are found on sidewalks throughout Berlin and recall the prewar Potsdamer Platz. The grillage accommodates drainage, earthen vaults for trees, and the distribution of an electrical grid for shows and exhibitions. The main stripes of the plaza paving follow one of the complex angles of the building. At another of the architectural angles a series of lozenge-shaped metal plates is set within the cobble band; when electrified, the plates glow in an unusual color.

Off center of the main plaza axis, a large stepped crescent of boxwood draws attention to the Cineplex lobby, which lies below the plaza level. Overlapping the opening is a circular reflecting pool with a glass bottom on the cantilevered section. The design draws the eye down to the theaters below, while from the lower lobby, theatergoers look up through the skylight and the transparent pool to the complex tent structure above.

Stainless steel bench lights in the form of circular segments line the entry passageways from the surrounding sidewalks and the subway plaza. In the entryway leading to the Tiergarten is a sculptural playground made of bright red padded plastic. In the courtyard formed by the curving cobbled service drive and the headquarters building lies a boxwood parterre that emphasizes the dynamic angles of the architecture. Beyond the Neue Potsdamerstrasse, a proposed radiating bosque of linden trees will bring the forest of the Tiergarten to the edge of Sony Center.

Early model of cantilevered pool

Landscape plan

1   Metal and cobble plaza
2   Pool
3   Stepped hedge
4   Subway plaza
5   Proposed Tiergarten park
6   Sony hedge garden
7   Inner street

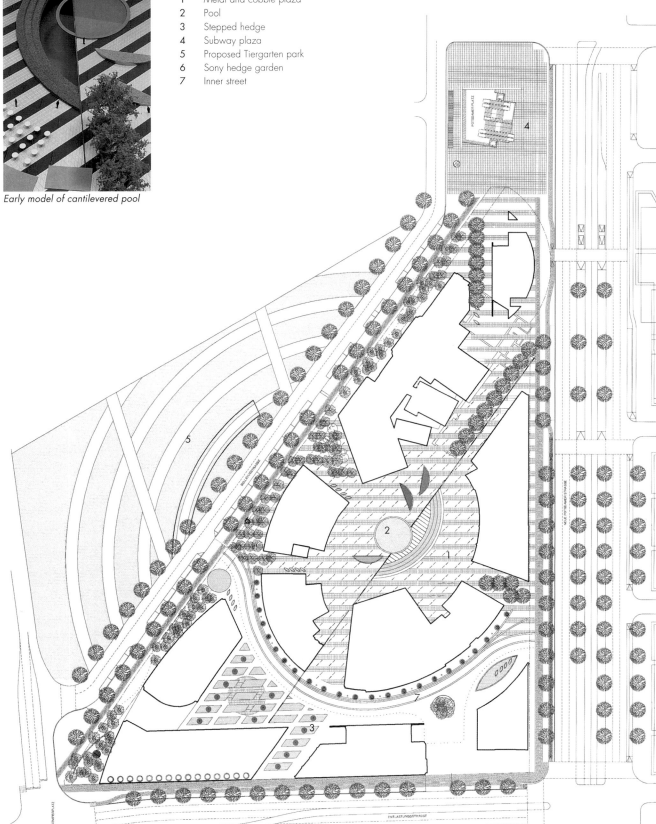

90

top
Stepped hedge and glass cantilevered pool

right
Looking up through the pool from
the theater lobby

top

Plaza in the daytime

Night view with electric plates

bottom

Steel grate and traditional

cobble paving

Birch grove at pedestrian entry

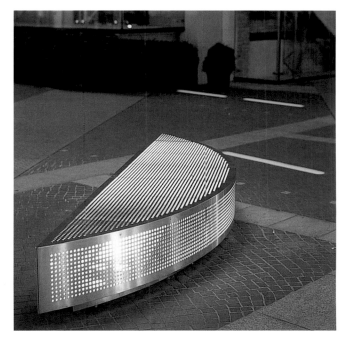

top
Interior street defined by bollards
Sony Headquarters entry garden

bottom
Soft plastic play sculpture
Lantern bench

Stanford University
Center for Clinical Science Research
Palo Alto, California

As a consultant to Foster and Partners, PWP designed the landscape within and around a new cancer-research center at Stanford University. The building is formed by two separate wings with banks of semicircular glass offices overlooking a central atrium topped by delicate steel arbors, which extend outward beyond the wings.

The atrium, which provides the building with an outdoor entry space and a terrace for an outdoor café, is paved with elongated concrete bricks of golden yellow. The metal grill of the arbors projects a delicate pattern of shadows onto the bricks and gives the atrium the feeling of a shaded garden room. At its center the terrace drops to a lower level, letting light into the offices and rooms below. An irregular row of forest bamboo runs the length of the atrium at both levels—a linear green scrim that visually separates the banks of offices without closing them in.

The entry steps and ramp lead down from the atrium to a paved and planted plaza that connects the building at grade to the entrance of the Beckman Center and the major pedestrian paths to the rest of the medical school and the main campus. The center is respectful of the adjacent hospital building designed by Edward Durrell Stone and contrasts with the more solid Beckman Center, to which it is connected at the second floor by a pedestrian bridge.

The east-facing laboratory windows overlook a new sculpture garden planted with hedges and live oaks and furnished with benches. The garden floor consists of lawn and an irregular pattern of pavement and gravel squares that protect the existing water-sensitive trees. A gravel moat and path run the length of the north building beneath the canopy to connect the entry plaza to historic Governor's Lane, which passes directly behind the building.

right
Sculpture garden with existing
live oaks

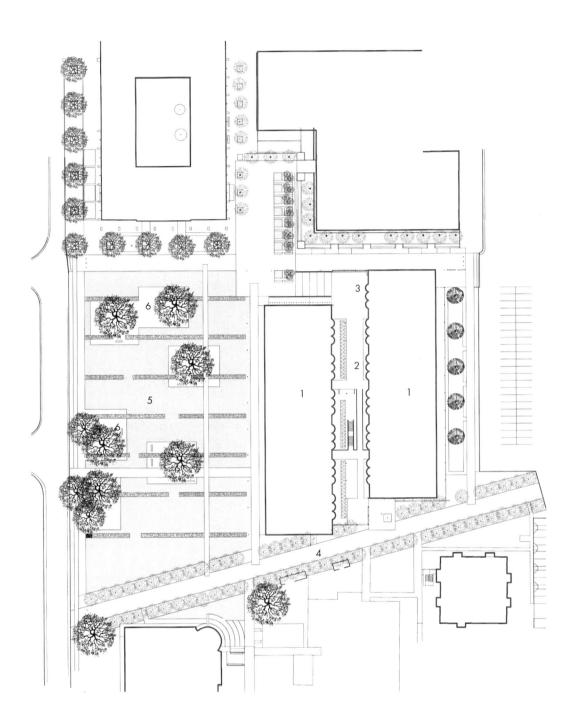

Landscape plan

1   Research buildings
2   Atrium
3   Café
4   Governor's Lane
5   Sculpture garden
6   Existing oaks

top

Café at atrium

Bamboo in steel lattice

bottom

Hedges and sculpture garden

Gravel beds to preserve live oaks

One North Wacker Drive
Chicago, Illinois

Pedestrian park with stone benches

98

The landscape for a fifty-two-story office tower in downtown Chicago, designed by Lohan Caprille Goettsch Architects, is a forty-foot-wide protected linear way that runs for a block along the side of the building. This pedestrian passage—West Madison Street—can be seen through the parallel glazed wall of the building's lobby. It ends at the rear of the building on North Franklin Street, where a small square serves as an outdoor terrace for a street-level restaurant.

Vaults running just below the sidewalk level made conventional tree wells impossible—a problem solved by specially formed hemispherical armatures that sustain ground-cover growth and allow the root balls of the street trees to remain above ground. The raised tree wells are placed thirty feet apart along the edge of the street. Carved stone benches provide comfortable seating and extend the architectural scale of the lobby out to the street.

The pavement at the outdoor base of the building is made of flat flamed-granite cobbles, further reinforcing the human scale of the promenade and terrace. (This is the first use of a cobble pavement in new construction in Chicago.) Custom-designed lights alternate with the trees of the linear park.

The terrace at the North Franklin Street entrance to the building contains three large bench planters, each with a treeless hemisphere floating in a pool of water. The reflection on the still surface of the pool turns each mound into a perfect sphere. Flowerbeds and flowering fruit trees transform the space into a welcome outdoor lunch venue.

right
Raised hemispherical armatures in planters

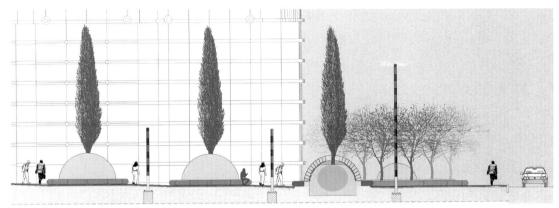

Section through raised hemispherical planters

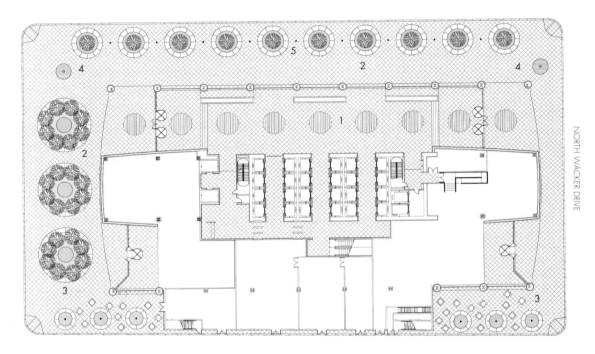

NORTH WACKER DRIVE

Landscape plan

1   Lobby
2   Sidewalk park
3   Dining park
4   Mist fountain
5   Raised planters

top right
Flowering grove and reflecting pools
bottom right
Stone benches and cobbled paving

Pixar Animation Studios

Emeryville, California

When Steve Jobs, chief executive officer of Apple Computer and Pixar Animation Studios, and John Lasseter, executive vice president of Pixar, decided to move their studios from leased space in Point Richmond to larger quarters of their own, they chose a site owned for many years by the Del Monte Company, producer of the fruit salad familiar to most of us from childhood. The first of several buildings, a high-tech structure designed by Bohlin Cywinski Jackson, has special foundations and generators to ensure continued production, even through major earthquakes. The character of the building is, nevertheless, intended to abstractly recall Emeryville's industrial past.

The twenty-acre park takes the form of a sculpted rolling lawn forested with a number of native and exotic species, including Monterey cypress, European beech, live oak, and cottonwood. At the pedestrian entrance, an allée of sycamore is bounded on one side by the park and on the other by a series of garden squares planted with a variety of roses. Inside the gate, flowering apple orchards border the entrance drive.

As the center of this working campus for Pixar's generally young employees, the park includes a swimming pool, a grass playing field, a basketball court, an amphitheater, groups of benches and tables, and a jogging trail. The first-phase surface-parking area is planted with rows of quick-growing Italian poplar and laid out to accommodate increments of future structural parking.

Raised forested edge   *Soccer field*   *Lookout garden*

Section through the park

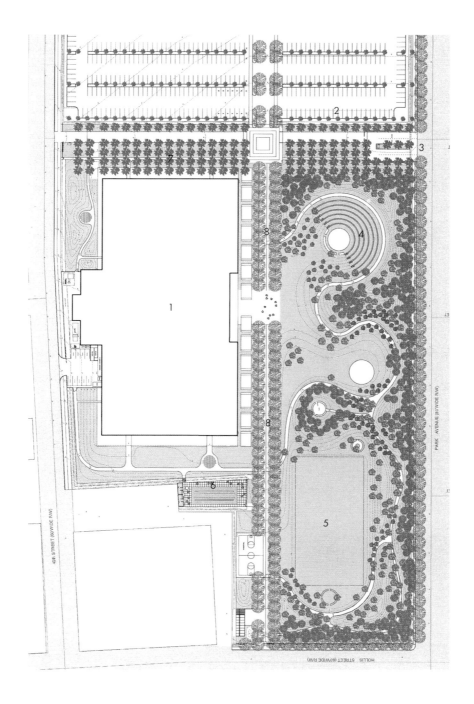

1   First studio
2   Parking
3   Entry
4   Amphitheater
5   Field
6   Pool
7   Orchards
8   Main walk

Amphitheater   *Entry drive with orchard*

104

Brick-and-grass amphitheater

top

Main pathway with plane trees

Patio

bottom

Winding path

Amphitheater

Triangle Park

St. Louis, Missouri

Rapid-transit station

Walk from plaza to station

Triangle Park in downtown St. Louis is an attempt to achieve the presence of the great Baroque water and light displays by modern means. A gift to St. Louis from the Gateway Foundation, the park provides plaza space for the Kiel Center, a sports, concert, and convention venue that was unfortunately designed without adjacent outdoor space. A path connects the plaza portion of the park to a new rapid-transit station at the bottom of a gentle hill. A series of cast-stone benches with lights illuminates the path.

The semicircular street-side plaza, which also acts as a gateway to the arena, is formed by ten large fog-walls, fourteen feet by fourteen feet by three feet. Each consists of a sandblasted stainless steel frame covered by thirty-six panels of punched stainless steel plates.

In addition to the manifold for a mist fountain, each tablet contains an armature of colored fluorescent lights. The yellow, blue, and red lights can be programmed to produce solid colors, stripes, and secondary colors as well as the colors of athletic teams; they can also be choreographed for various seasonal celebrations. At night the fog at the center and the colored light at the edges merge in a magic blur, a radiating presence slightly obscured by the perforated scrim of the plates.

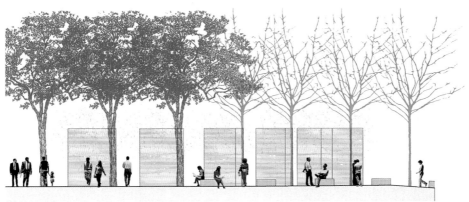

Perforated stainless steel fountain wall

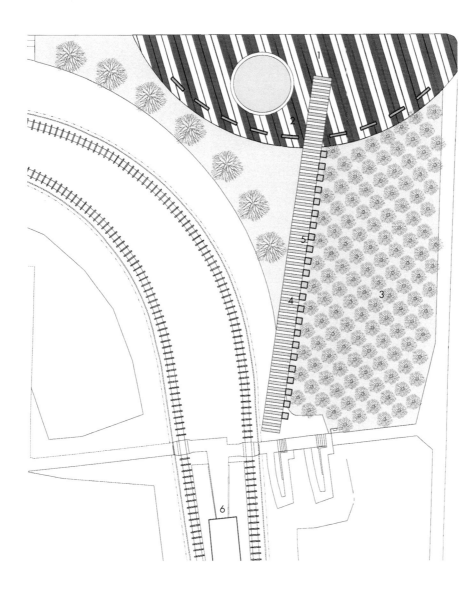

1   Fountain plaza
2   Fountain wall
3   Orchard
4   Path
5   Bench lights
6   Station

Plaza at night

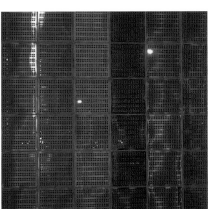

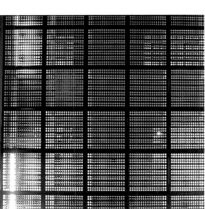

Light changes within fountain walls

Stanford University Schwab Center
Graduate School of Business Housing
Palo Alto, California

Palm court from above

In 1995 Ricardo Legorreta of Legorreta Arquitectos and PWP won a competition to design a new type of teaching facility for the Stanford School of Business. The design was for an intimate residential college for a short-term, intensified program leading to a master's degree in business. The buildings include residential rooms, informal study rooms, lecture facilities, kitchen and dining areas, and lounges—all clustered around a series of complex spaces of varying sizes, scales, and degrees of specificity of use.

Entry is through the great wooden front door into an office reception lounge that leads directly outdoors, down a series of shaded but open corridors. To the left, a courtyard holds geometrically placed palms and tiled fountains that direct the gaze upward to the open sky. The central corridor continues through a series of courtyards to the dining and meeting halls.

Crossing the major spine, additional covered corridors lead north and south to two other major open spaces. One, completely painted deep blue, extends down into a large pool surrounded by willow and fern. To the south, two-story student rooms surround a large grassed courtyard planted with dark green conifers, including clusters of pine and a formal bosque of cypress. Adjacent to each of these major spaces, convenient smaller courts and alcoves provide secure parking for bicycles, the preferred vehicle on campus.

The dining patio is furnished with large wooden outdoor tables and chairs and an orchard of pear trees. In the opposite court stands a grid of historic stone columns salvaged from Stanford University buildings damaged in the Loma Prieta earthquake of 1989.

Palm court with tile bench-fountains

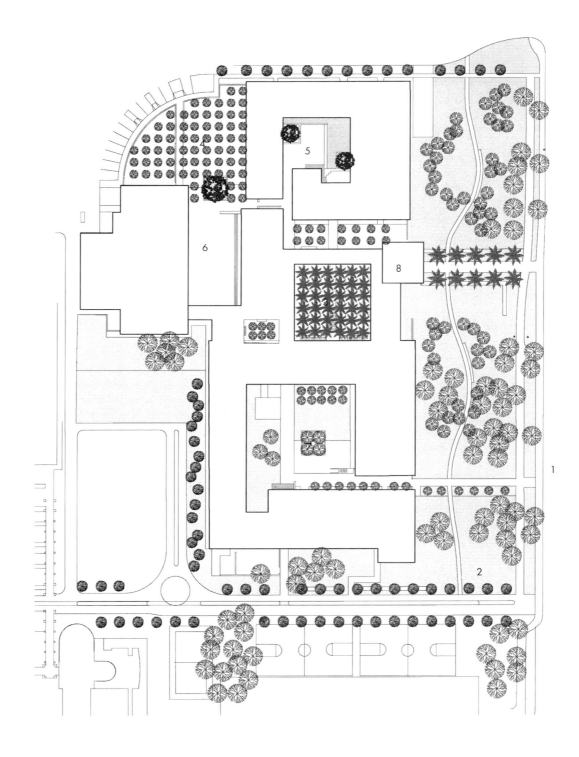

Landscape plan

1   Serra Mall
2   Linear park
3   Palm court
4   Dining orchard
5   Pool court
6   Column court
7   Residential garden
8   Lobby

top
Blue water garden
Planting with red walls

bottom
Plaza with stone columns saved
from the 1989 earthquake
Bicycle parking

Copia: The American Center for Wine, Food, and Arts

Napa, California

Demonstration gardens

Each year more than 4.9 million visitors come to the California wine country from all corners of the world to sample the fine cabernets, zinfandels, pinot noirs, chardonnays, and merlots; to dine in the many extraordinary valley restaurants; and to take the wine train from Napa to Calistoga. In 1993 James Stewart Polshek and PWP were awarded a commission to design a new museum and museum garden in Napa. The client was a newly endowed nonprofit institution, Copia, a name that suggests agricultural abundance. The active advisory board includes Robert Mondavi and many of his winemaking colleagues from around the world as well as such world-famous chefs as Alice Waters.

The new center would offer an intense and sustained public program dedicated to the lively culture of California. Demonstrations would be offered in the arts, in the growing and harvesting of grapes, and in the preparation of fine food and wine. Since the Napa Valley has, on average, 300 dry, sunny days a year, with temperatures ranging from 38 degrees to 82 degrees, much of the program could be outside with elegant spaces for dining, concerts, and lectures located throughout the 11.5-acre site.

The new museum lies in an oxbow of the Napa River and is edged on three sides by water. Although the U.S. Army Corps of Engineers is modifying the river channel to eliminate occasional flooding, the building was placed on the highest ground of the site, and the gardens and their river edges have been carefully designed to cope with rising river levels.

The main entry walk is formed as an 825-foot-long gravel path lined with tall poplars and paved in golden decomposed granite. On its east side, a stepped linear reflecting pond gestures 250 feet to the museum's entrance. The walk divides the garden from the parking areas, which are planted with varietal grapevines and native grasses. The display gardens lie on both sides of First Street.

An outdoor amphitheater and several dining terraces lie adjacent to the demonstration restaurants. Framed by stone walls and divided into smaller plots by grass pathways, the gardens are filled with a cornucopia of California fruits, vegetables, and ornamental garden plants and flowers. The small plots are constantly replanted so that frequent visitors will enjoy a rich and changing display. Extensive outdoor cooking facilities are located in the lower garden area.

right
Linear reflecting pool at entry

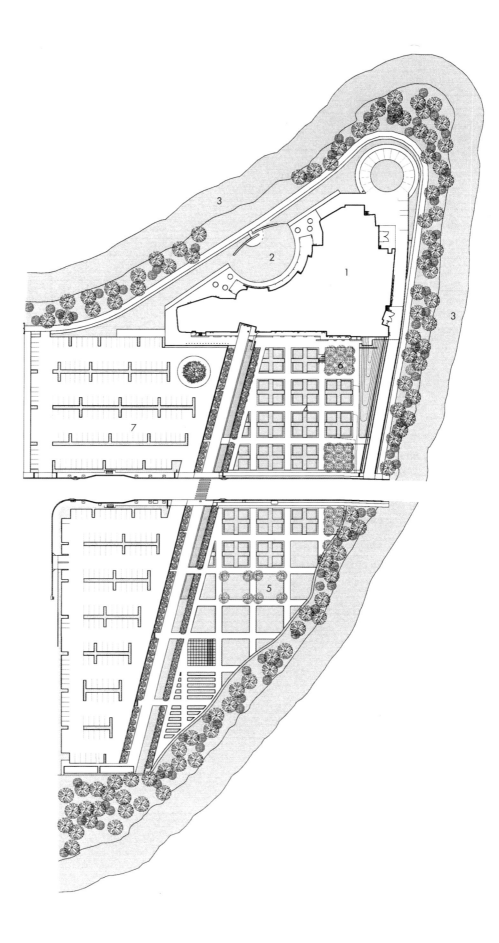

Landscape plan

1 Museum building
2 Amphitheater
3 Napa River
4 Upper gardens
5 Lower gardens
6 Dining terrace
7 Parking

top
A variety of changing display
gardens including grasses,
vegetables, cutting flowers,
vines, and flowering shrubs

page 118
Decomposed-granite path
with stone-lined beds

page 119
Shaded dining terrace
with specimen olive trees

Circular Park
Nishi Harima, Japan

In 1994 PWP prepared detailed landscape plans and construction documents for a circular town park at the intersection of the two major roads of Nishi Harima, a new town with a master plan by Arata Isozaki and PWP that was begun in 1990. The park physically and symbolically marks the beginning of the new town.

Terraced from the intersection to the civic spaces above, the park contains a grand stone promenade, a children's play area, a stylized bamboo forest, a large pond, and seating areas. The terraces are furnished with walks, benches, lights, and a circular poplar hedgerow. At the main corner of the park stands a monument of stones laid without mortar in the form of a half sphere.

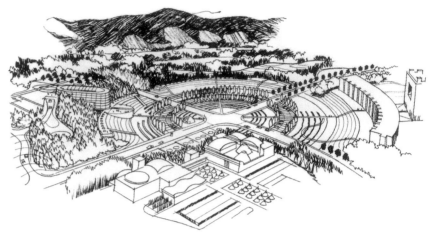

Sketch of Circular Park

The mound, which glows from within at night, memorializes the new town, which is built adjacent to a huge supercollider. (See pages 180–181 for the planning of Nishi Harima Science Garden City.) Along the upper terrace stretches a line of monumental vertical fake stones, which also glow from within at night to form a semicircle of giant lanterns.

The park incorporates the town conference center and *ryokan*, also designed by Isozaki and PWP, and an existing golf course as well as sites for a future concert hall, initial low-cost housing, and a shopping area.

Newly planted Circular Park

Promenade of monumental stones
day and night

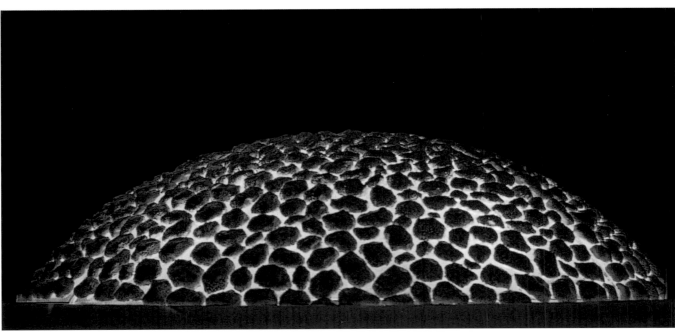

Town symbol
day and night

Clark Center for Biomedical
Engineering and Sciences
Stanford University
Palo Alto, California

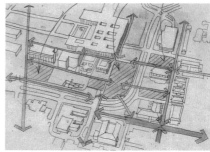

Main circulation diagram

124   At the southwest corner of Stanford's Medical Center campus stands one of the largest and most experimental buildings in the history of the university. It is no accident that the new Clark Center, designed by Foster and Partners, is located in this position, at the meeting point of the engineering-school complex, the biological-sciences group, and the medical-research campus, for it is part of a new approach to research that is based on overlapping several university departments. In this case physics, bio-engineering, biochemistry, computer science, and medical research are all housed in one research building, among the first of its kind in the academic United States.

Clark Center serves as a gateway for pedestrian movement to, and through, the medical complex, and the rectilinear building was raised on a grass berm to increase the apparent size of the lawn and to visually relieve the relatively small site. Campus Drive, the major postwar automobile route on campus, was rerouted and reengineered, and part of the major utility infrastructure was moved. The parkway character of Campus Drive—which catered almost exclusively to cars—has been changed to a more urban configuration that facilitates pedestrian movement toward the main campus.

At the Clark Center a voluptuous curving interior wall forms an open courtyard. Open stairways lead to a series of continuous exterior open hallways accessing the building at many points. This curving outdoor pedestrian superstructure overlooks the partially paved, partially grassed courtyard below. Fifteen robinia trees reach up to visually engage the superstructure. Beneath the grove, stepping stones connect the two curving paths, and a series of monolithic, roughly carved solid granite blocks gesturally reinforce the sense of movement through the courtyard. Some of these blocks come together to make benches for the informal seating that encourages collegial conversation, while the terrace recalls a European street-side café. Behind the cafeteria to the west, a grassed terrace surrounded by a grove of redwoods provides outdoor privacy for meetings, dining, and parties. From everywhere inside the courtyard, the trees and stairs draw the viewer's eyes upward to the extraordinary piece of sky shaped by the extended overhang of the elegant roof.

Adjacent to the central courtyard are meeting rooms, a sunken auditorium, and a restaurant and café with tables that drift out into the court. At grade level is a dining plaza with an outdoor stage and a stairway leading down to the auditorium. To the east, a curving lawn extends out to the existing Dean's Lawn, which is studded with mature live oaks. A curved stone pathway follows the glass building wall, connecting the stairs and various meeting rooms at grade. There is no single front door.

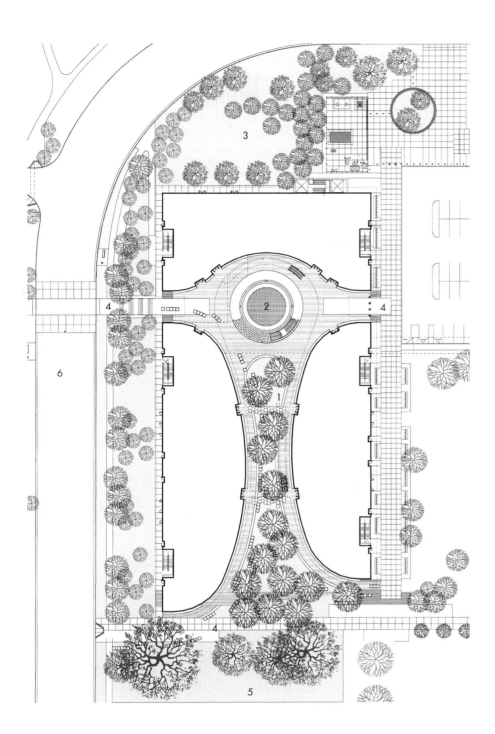

View along main hospital path with bikes

Entry from Dean's Lawn

View from Campus Drive

Landscape plan

1 Courtyard
2 Stage
3 Function lawn
4 Entry
5 Dean's Lawn
6 Realigned campus drive

126

Main walk with split-stone
benches and stone paving

top
Courtyard with stage and café

middle
Curved lawn
Fedestrian bridge

bottom
East steps
Meeting space
Stone benches

Stanford University Medical Center
Parking Garage
Palo Alto, California

Garage overview

Pasteur Drive connects Sand Hill Road to the Stanford University Hospital, designed by Edward Durrell Stone, and Forecourt Fountain, designed by Thomas Church. An earlier planning study by PWP called for a two-block orchard of olive trees that would lead to the more formal forecourt. Diagonally crossing the orchard would be a reconstruction of Governor's Lane, a historic riding trail formerly lined with rows of mature eucalyptus, now changed to sycamore. When it was determined that the parking structure should be below ground, PWP was asked to design a landscape over the garage that would retain the sense of openness and the earlier agricultural character of the campus. A minimum soil depth was desired for cost reasons and so that the garage could be as near the existing grade as possible.

Just as the Pasteur entrance in the PWP master plan was designed to be reminiscent of the earlier farm atmosphere of the campus, so the new garage design references agricultural history by means of seat-high wooden walls, which recall the wooden slews, water coolers, and agricultural retaining walls of early California ranches and farms. These seat walls, made of ipe wood, which weathers naturally to a soft silvery gray, form large separated boxes that create a rustic park of alleys and courts. In the boxes that lie over the garage structure, the shallow soil is planted with a complex mix of native California meadow grasses and wildflowers that bloom throughout the spring and the long Palo Alto summer. In fall, the grasses turn the golden color that is a hallmark of open California grasslands. This "boxed meadow," ambiguously synthetic and natural, provides a major new accessible open space for the Medical Center campus. Specimen live oaks relate to the native oaks that have been preserved throughout the campus.

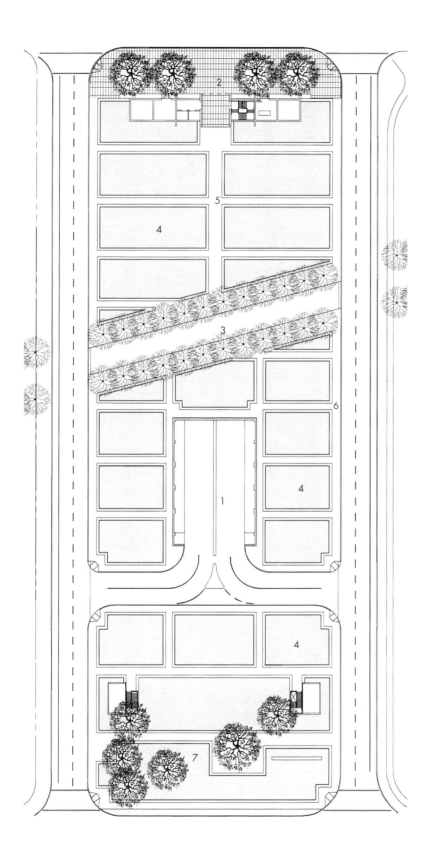

Decomposed-granite walkway

Wood matrix bench

Native grasses

129

Garage garden plan

1   Automobile entry and exit
2   Pedestrian entry and exit
3   Governor's Lane (replanted)
4   Wild-grass beds (boxes)
5   Wood benches
6   Consolidated gravel paths
7   Replanted live oaks

Nasher Foundation
Sculpture Center
Dallas, Texas

Fountain at lily pond

Architect Renzo Piano selected PWP as the landscape architect for a sculpture garden and small museum that together will house one of the world's most important private collections of modern sculpture. The client is Raymond Nasher, who built up the collection with his wife, Patsy R. Nasher, and continued collecting after her death in 1988. The Nasher family decided to build the sculpture center as a gift to the citizens of Dallas.

The sculpture garden is designed as an outdoor gallery that can hold between twenty and thirty pieces, some permanently and some in changing displays. Among the pieces included in the garden are works by Pablo Picasso, Alexander Calder, Henry Moore, Auguste Rodin, Barbara Hepworth, Joan Miro, Naum Gabo, George Segal, Joel Shapiro, Roy Lichtenstein, and Magdalena Abakanowicz, with large pieces by Richard Serra, Mark di Suvero, Jonathan Borofsky, and a new room piece by James Turrell. The great weight of some of the pieces and the movement of sculpture in and out of the garden necessitated the invention of a special soil that drains perfectly without catch basins, is strong enough to hold the weight loads, and can support the growth of a special resilient grass turf as well as many large specimen trees. To allow as much flexibility as an indoor museum space, pavement was kept to a minimum while meeting public ADA requirements. Stone plinths distribute flexible systems of lighting, sound, security, and irrigation throughout the garden and provide casual seating and additional sites for smaller pieces of sculpture.

The museum faces Flora Street, the central spine of the Dallas Arts District. Piano conceived of the building as a parallel series of "archaeological" walls directing sight and movement from Flora Street through the delicately glazed building and out to the garden. The side walls of the garden, which are opened up by transparent gates and windows that allow glimpses of the garden from Olive and Harwood streets, extend this concept. A live-oak allée, hedges, and the stone plinths, all composed along the long axis of the garden, form a series of continuous linear spaces. An irregular orchard of cedar elm creates a counterpoint to the longitudinal lines, forming spaces that vary in size and scale and are suitable for the display of a wide range of sculpture.

A broad stone terrace and steps connect the museum to the garden, continuing the plane that flows from Flora Street through the building. Tables and chairs from the museum café spill onto the terrace. A fountain of fine sparkling jets originating in the garden wall rains into a seventy-foot-long pool planted with water lilies. The falling water catches the sunlight and masks sound from the Olive Street traffic. Between the outer garden walls and the end walls of the museum tight groves of forest bamboo reinforce the linear composition while subtly screening views into the garden.

At the foot of the garden, two pools with lines of white waterjets and a linear planting of rushes draw visitors through the garden and mask the noise from the sunken freeway that lies beyond. Parallel to the pools, a wooden boardwalk connects the two main longitudinal stone paths. The Turrell room is embedded in an eight-foot-high stepped mound behind the pool area. The mound, which provides additional sound protection, is overplanted with a loose grove of pine that forms a backdrop for a drift of flowering crepe myrtle.

The paving of the garden paths, entry plaza, terrace, and stair is a flame-finish dark Verde Fontaine granite with green highlights, a color that resembles the deep green of the live oaks, cherry hedge, and magnolia trees along Harwood Street. The steel bollards at the entry plaza and the metal work of fences and rails are a soft gray that matches the metal of the building curtain wall and the cast-metal grill of the translucent ceiling.

Henry Moore

Auguste Rodin

Magdalena Abakanowicz

Alexander Calder

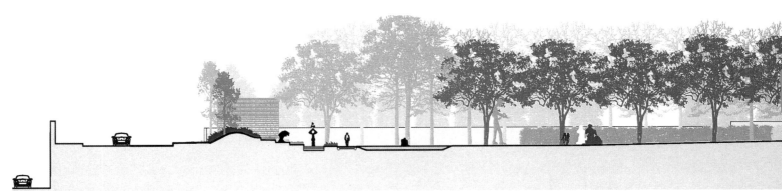

Section through sculpture garden and amphitheater   *Stepped garden and pool*   *Live-oak allée*

Section   *Stepped garden*   *Pool*   *Jonathan Borofsky*   *Hedge*   *Cedar-elm rooms*

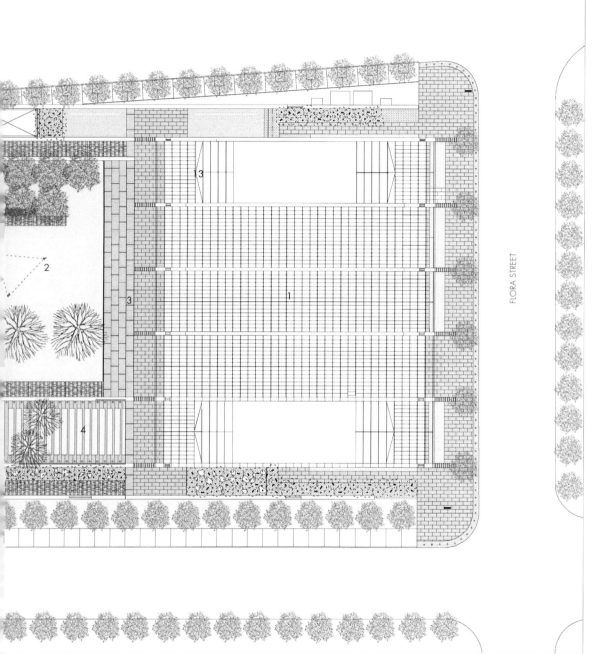

FLORA STREET

Landscape plan

1	Museum
2	Great lawn
3	Porch and stairs
4	Amphitheater
5	Live-oak allée
6	Pool
7	Boardwalk
8	Turrell room
9	Steppec garden
10	Cedar-elm orchard rooms
11	Hedges
12	Stone walk
13	Café
14	Asian museum

14

OLIVE STREET

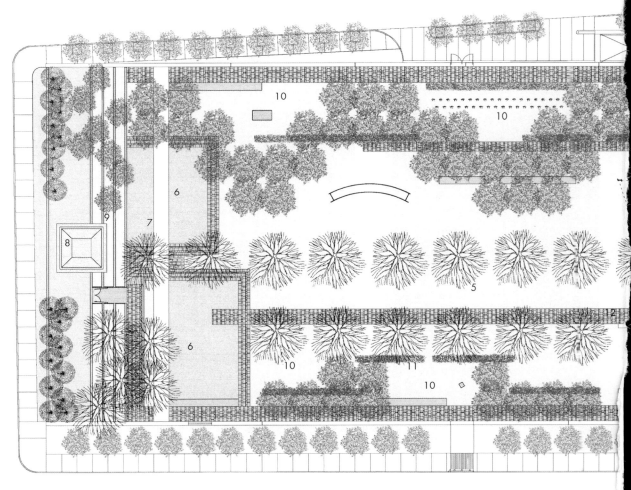

10

10

6

9

7

8

5

6

12

10

11

10

NORTH HARWOOD STREET

DALLAS MUSEUM OF ART

Roy Lichtenstein

Scott Burton

Richard Serra

George Segal

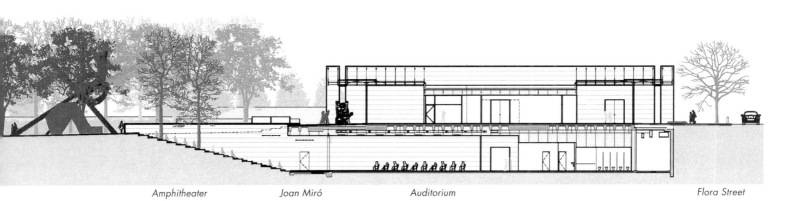

Amphitheater   *Joan Miró*   *Auditorium*   *Flora Street*

Mark di Suvero   *Porch*   *Museum*   *Entry plaza*

Aerial view looking south

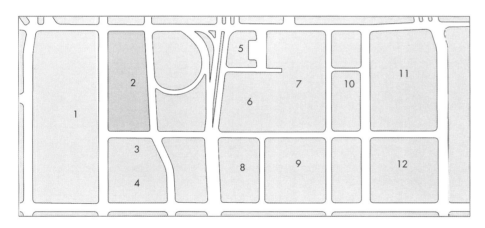

Arts District plan

1	Dallas Museum of Art
2	Nasher Foundation Sculpture Center
3	Crow Asian Art Collection
4	Trammell Crow Center
5	Morton H. Meyerson Symphony Square
6	Symphony garden
7	Annette Strauss Artist Square
8	Cathedral Santuario de Guadalupe
9	Arts District Parking Garage
10	Arts District Theater (temporary)
11	Booker T. Washington High School for the Performing and Visual Arts
12	Dallas Center for Performing Arts

133

left top
Sculpture garden with pools
left bottom
Boardwalk and rush garden

Main path and live-oak allée
looking toward the building

left
Stepped garden, boardwalk, and
fountain pools

top
Main axis with a Barbara Hepworth
sculpture and sculptures by Rodin,
Calder, and DuBuffet beyond

bottom
The garden in snow

pages 136-137
Oak allée with Barbara Hepworth,
Auguste Rodin, and Scott Burton
sculptures

PROJECTS IN PROGRESS

IF THE CONCEPTS OF A GIVEN PROJECT ARE TO BE REALIZED, THE THREE-DIMENSIONALITY AND THE FABRICATION TECHNIQUES MUST BE CLEARLY COMMUNICATED TO REVIEWERS AND BUILDERS. THOUGHTFUL DOCUMENTATION, NECESSARY FOR THE DETAILED UNDERSTANDING OF THE PROPOSED WORK, IS THE BASIS FOR CONSTRUCTION REVIEW AND SUPERVISION. ALONG WITH NORMAL ENGINEERING CONSTRUCTION, LANDSCAPE ARCHITECTURE DEALS WITH THE INSTALLATION OF LIVING PLANTS, WHICH REQUIRE THE CAREFUL BUILDING OF SUCH SUPPORT SYSTEMS AS IRRIGATION AND DRAINAGE AS WELL AS THE COMPLEX COMPOSITION OR MODIFICATION OF PARTICULAR SOILS, BOTH CHEMICALLY AND MECHANICALLY. ALL OF NATURE'S FORCES CANNOT—AND PERHAPS SHOULD NOT—BE STRUCTURALLY RESISTED, BUT CALCULATIONS OF THESE

IMPRECISE MOVEMENTS ARE IMPORTANT, PARTICULARLY WHEN DEALING WITH RECLAIMED LAND AND WITH LANDSCAPE CONSTRUCTION OVER ENGINEERED STRUCTURES—AN INCREASING SHARE OF OUR URBANIZING ENVIRONMENTS. OF COURSE, LANDSCAPE ARCHITECTS CANNOT ANTICIPATE ALL CONSTRUCTION PROBLEMS. SURVEYS, LAWS, REGULATIONS, AND TECHNIQUES CHANGE CONTINUALLY AND VARY GREATLY THROUGHOUT THE WORLD. TO DEAL WITH THESE AND OTHER ISSUES, INCLUDING CLIENT, PROFESSIONAL, AND PUBLIC LIABILITY, PWP PUTS SPECIAL EMPHASIS ON THE CONSTRUCTION DRAWINGS. OVER THE PAST FORTY YEARS PWP HAS INCREASED ITS INVESTMENT IN THESE ARTICLES OF SERVICE FROM ROUGHLY TWENTY-FIVE PERCENT TO MORE THAN HALF OF OUR EFFORTS.

American Embassy
Beijing, China

Hand-laid stone   *Native brick*   *Lotus*

140 Working with Craig Hartman of Skidmore, Owings & Merrill, PWP won a competition to design the gardens for the American Embassy in Beijing. The new compound occupies a 40,000-square-meter site in the embassy district. The site design includes a continuous stone-and-concrete wall completely surrounding the compound. The outside of the wall is smooth, the inside is planted with ivy (Parthenocissus tricuspidata). There are three entrances to the embassy: one for the consulate; one for the embassy's formal entry; and one through the parking structure for staff. Outside the consulate entry and at the corner are small parks and waiting areas with raised planters that include benches. Parking for guest bicycles is adjacent to the corner, and parking for staff bicycles is outside the wall on two sides of the parking garage.

Two wooden bridges cross a traditional lotus pond that lies behind the compound gates; one bridge is at the consular entry for pedestrians, the other at the embassy entrance for pedestrians and automobiles. Beyond the embassy bridge, an arrival plaza, paved with antique Chinese stones and lined with a band of rough natural stones, offers a warm but dignified welcome. In the center of the plaza stands a raised grass circle with a cluster of low trees and the embassy flagpole.

At the corner of the pond, the lotus planting opens up to reveal a fountain made of oxygen jets that aerate the pond and create a white bubbling figure on its surface. Chinese weeping willows (Salix babylonica) line the south side of the pond, which is visible from the entry bridges and from outside by means of flush glass windows at the folded corner of the perimeter wall. Hedged gardens with central grass mounds and spreading specimen trees occupy the remaining three corners of the enclosed yard. A broad path of decomposed granite with periodic bench-height stone walls surrounds three sides of the complex inside the security wall. Clusters of traditional water-formed Chinese stones stand at the pond ends of the path.

Rows of American elms planted on either side of the path form an allée on the north side of the building cluster, which opens to a large lawn space intended for major embassy parties. At the west end of the great lawn lie three large circular beds filled with American roses. At the east end of the lawn a grove of columnar trees provides shade for a sitting area with benches. Around the corner from the columnar grove, a bosque of lacebark pine creates a visual background for the interior courtyard. Across the pedestrian bridge, a large covered porch—paved with antique

Chinese stone and holding another composition of major art stones—offers views of the pond and fountain to visitors waiting inside the gate.

Inside the building complex, a pedestrian "street," partially covered by an overhang, parallels a continuous linear grove of forest bamboo. Intimate courts are cut into the bamboo grove. They are defined by seat-high stone walls and furnished with outdoor tables and chairs. At one end of the pedestrian street a walled court, created by a lawn surrounded by flowering cherry trees, can serve as a venue for smaller embassy functions and outdoor press briefings. The courtyard is to receive a major commissioned artwork. At the other end of the bamboo grove an informal plaza, All Seasons Court—paved with antique Chinese granite—serves the cafeteria, gymnasium, and recreation area. The family and social center of the complex, the court contains outdoor tables and chairs and a small grove of paperbark maple trees.

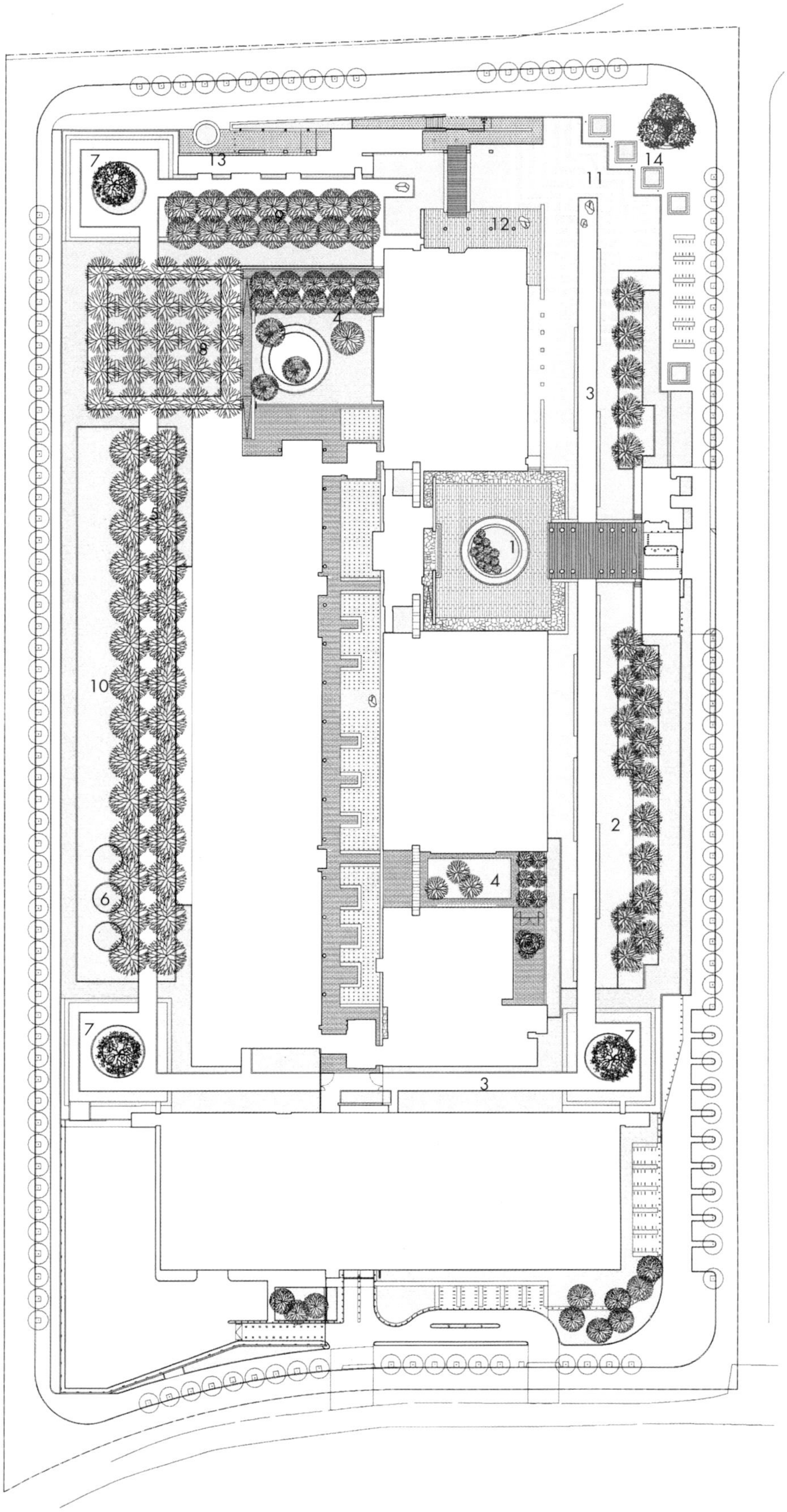

Landscape plan

1 Embassy arrival court
2 Lotus pool with willows
3 Pedestrian street
4 Cherry courtyard
5 Elm allée
6 Rose garden
7 Corner garden
8 Bosque
9 Pine grove
10 Great lawn
11 Chevron fcuntain
12 Consulate entry
13 Public waiting garden
14 Viewing wall

Model of moat garden at the consulate

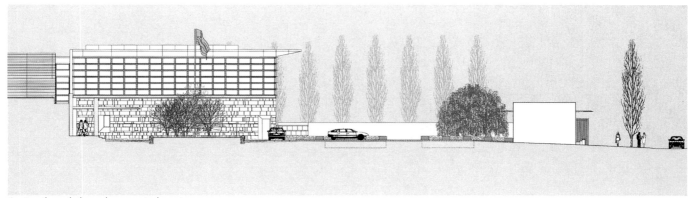

Section through the embassy arrival court

Section through the corner garden

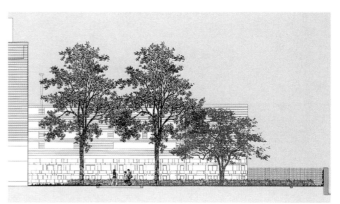

Section through the great lawn with elm allée

Bangkok Airport
Bangkok, Thailand

Temple precedent

144 For the new Bangkok airport, designed by the MJTA Consortium of Murphy/Jahn, Inc., TAMS Consultants, and Act Group Building, PWP proposed outdoor and indoor gardens to animate the arrival and departure routes for automobiles and two levels of pedestrian movement. The automobile portion of the design consists of landscapes at a large scale that can be perceived from a moving automobile. These include conventional linear high-speed highway plantings as well as several large geometric plantings that can be viewed at the slower speeds of arrival and during the search for parking. The plants include various palm, citrus, and tropical flowering trees.

In the interior of the airport two monumental gardens designed on a twenty-seven-square-meter module (135 by 108 meters) can be viewed by pedestrians when entering the airport at grade and leaving the airport on the floor above. Each of the gardens employs an element of water—an important aspect of Thailand's tropical landscape. The first of these is a modern version of a palace water garden with tens of thousands of small jets playing on a field of mosaic tiles reminiscent of splendid coverings of temples throughout Thailand. The mosaics are broken into elaborate three-dimensional colored squares with gold-tile trim, which are enriched by the bright reflections of the water. At the head of the fountain court stand three traditional Thai stupas, the center structure taller and more elaborately tiled than the other two. The monuments offer visitors a warm symbolic welcome from the king and royal house of Thailand.

The second garden speaks of the agricultural landscape of the country. Here, gridded walkways crisscross stylized rice paddies planted with various reeds and grasses in the traditional Thai formal pattern symbolizing nature, wind, fire, water, and growth. Across these paddies lumber a herd of elephants, the symbol of Thai royalty. More than twice the size of real Asian elephants, these monumental beasts are topiaries—wire armatures covered with climbing vines. Hundreds of chairs are sprinkled throughout both gardens.

Along the pedestrian fingers of the terminals, tropical gardens display the rich and varied flora of the region. Within these "jungle" gardens the discerning eye detects life-sized topiary sculptures of monkeys, apes, tigers, lions, and reptiles. Authentic monumental sculptures of traditional Thai gateway guards and warriors stand at the intersections of the pedestrian concourses protecting passengers and leading to airline gates.

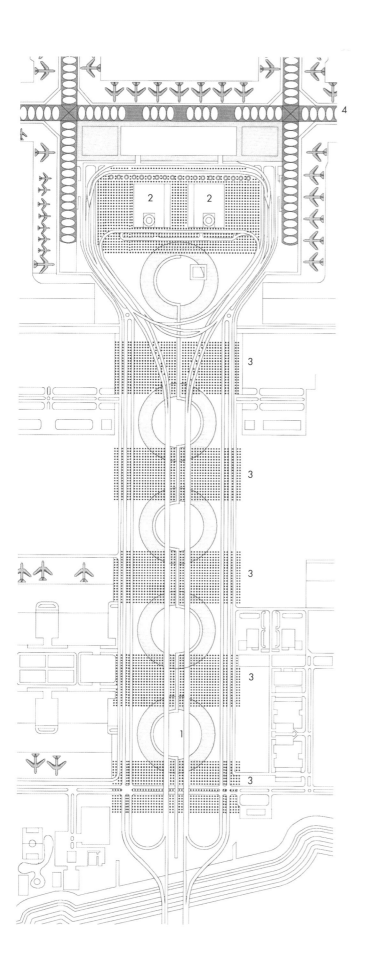

Airport arrival garden

Landscape plan

1 Arrival drive with citrus circles
2 Formal gardens
3 Palm orchards
4 Concourse

146

Tile-fountain courtyard with polychrome
tile and a thousand small jets

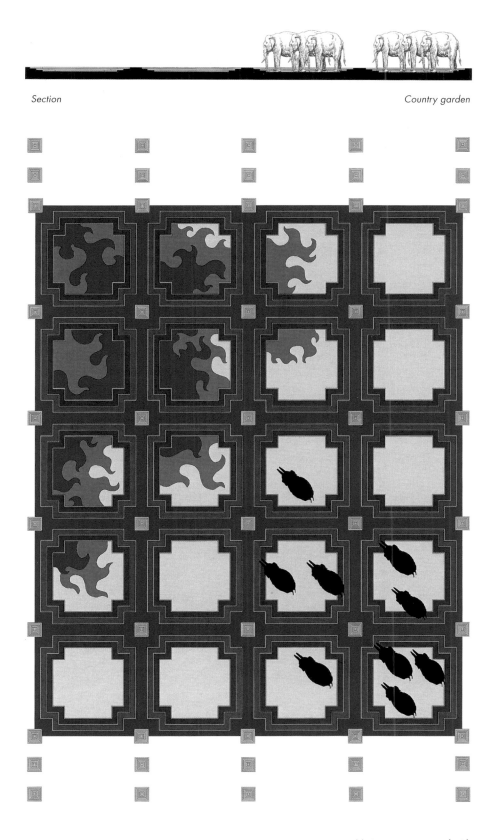

Section

Country garden

*Native-grass courtyard with
a herd of topiary elephants*

Deutsche Post Headquarters
Bonn, Germany

Pedestrian entry from park

Joinery at terrace

Cobbled automobile entrance plaza

148

The new headquarters of the Deutsche Post sits on a prominence overlooking the Rheinau, a large mature park at the edge of the Rhein River in Bonn, Germany. The building, designed by Helmut Jahn of Murphy/Jahn, Inc., is boat-shaped in plan. Its extraordinary glass curtain wall rises forty stories above a great terrace that overlooks and connects to the riverside park. The terrace is surfaced with broad stripes of grass, green marble, black granite cobbles, and perforated metal plates, which provide drainage access and display a random distribution of thousands of tiny fiber-optic lights. The striped paving pattern of the terrace continues through the lobby and ground floor of the building. At the entry of the building a large stone disk—alternately striped in black and white cobbles—stretches from streetside to underneath the glass entrance canopy.

To the right of the entry is a small VIP surface-parking lot bordered with stainless steel bollards. At the park side of the great terrace, perforated glass benches serve as lanterns along a public pedestrian path overlooking the park. The major parking area lies beneath the terrace in several stories of partially underground garage. At the rear of the terrace a major ramp and stairs made of diagonal concrete retaining walls and planting connect to the lower levels of the park. To the right of the ramp and stairs are more benches and a pedestrian bridge leading to a small restaurant structure within the park.

On the north side a broad path and stair are located within an existing allée that borders the park and leads to the river's edge. Below street level, a second terraced entrance to the building with a public post office connects to the allée. The smaller terrace features a quiet circular pool with black stone benches.

Grand terrace of stone, stainless steel, cobbles, and grass

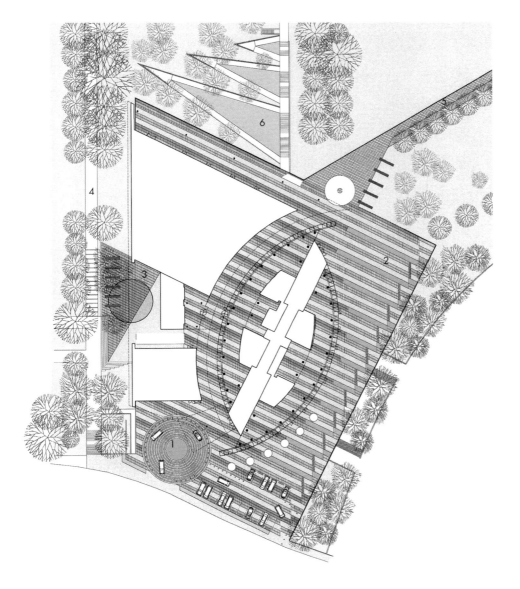

1   Arrival plaza
2   Grass, steel, and stone terrace
3   Lower post office garden
    with pool
4   Walk to Rhein River
5   Bridge to park
6   Stair and path to park

University of California
San Francisco, Mission Bay
San Francisco, California

A competition held in 1998 produced an overall master plan for a new forty-three-acre life-sciences campus for graduate teaching and research at the University of California, San Francisco (UCSF), to be built in the Mission Bay redevelopment area. The plan calls for an urban campus with open spaces available to students and faculty, the general public, and the surrounding neighborhood. Public streets allow automobile traffic through the campus. PWP was selected to do the detailed site planning and the landscape design for the first phase of the new campus, which includes buildings by Cesar Pelli and the Smith Group with ZGF Architects, as well as a student center and recreation facility by Legorreta Arquitectos.

The master plan proposed three major spaces—a campus green, a plaza, and an open playfield complex—plus a series of small adjacent squares or gardens at the entry to each building complex. Two major pedestrian streets—running from Third Street to Owens Street—connect the buildings and campus open spaces. The continuation of Fourteenth and Fifteenth streets through the campus as public roads requires a number of automobile and pedestrian entries and at-grade street crossings.

Since this is a new campus with no established faculty or student body, an extensive series of workshops with the campus architect and planner, faculty, staff, and student representatives from the UCSF Parnassus Heights campus helped PWP develop a detailed program and process the beginning site designs. Through use of representative images and models with movable symbols representing functions and spaces, participants in the workshops carefully developed the design and site vocabularies. Fortunately, the new site is located in a much warmer climate zone than the existing campus and the opportunity for open-space use is much greater.

The site is an industrial brownfield of largely historic fill above mud, requiring construction to be on pilings. Although the open campus sites have been substantially surcharged, some differential settlement may still occur; PWP therefore recommended flexible or unit paving, rusticated stone walls, and largely informal plantings that will not betray future earth movement.

Each tree-lined pedestrian street has a unique paving and planting scheme in order to be immediately recognizable throughout the campus. The campus green of grass and de-composed granite with pine-shaded edges, flowering accent trees, and open meadows allows informal athletics. (The playfields are scheduled for later phases.) A sculpted grass hill provides an outdoor gathering place and classroom while blocking street noise. Activities in the meeting and banquet rooms of the new student center can extend outdoors onto a generous terrace. Long walls of rusticated stone edge the terrace and provide informal seating at various places overlooking the green. Behind the student center a formal

tree-shaded VIP court is a drop-off point for taxis and automobiles. Truck service to buildings—a function not dealt with in the master plan—has been worked into several of the street entry areas and disguised to minimize any negative visual impact. Screened bicycle parking is distributed throughout all campus phases.

Although the Mission Bay developer provided the public-street planting, PWP reinforced the edge areas inside the walks with additional trees and shrubs. The palette and application of the landscape materials will be extended through future phases as the campus grows to completion over time.

The first building in the second phase will be a block of student housing by Skidmore, Owings & Merrill. It will be built around public and private courtyards featuring extensive grass, shrubbery, and trees. Several parking structures are soon to follow. On the plaza side of the housing, there will be restaurants and shopping services with outdoor café seating. A major two-part sculpture by Richard Serra has been proposed for the stone-paved plaza. On the opposite side of the plaza, additional student services and shops will be built into the street level of a second parking structure.

Automobile and pedestrian gateways mark the many campus entries and pedestrian crosswalks. Rusticated stone walls and campus markers carry signage and way-faring information. The campus has an extensive open-space lighting system to facilitate nighttime activities.

Aerial view of the site

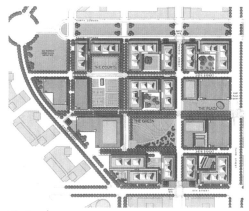

Master plan

Phase One landscape plan

A   Student union
B   Research building
C   Parking
D   Student housing
1   Central green
2   Student union terrace
3   Amphitheater
4   Main campus walk
5   Campus plaza
6   Student housing courtyard
7   Campus entry
8   VIP entry
9   Richard Serra sculptures

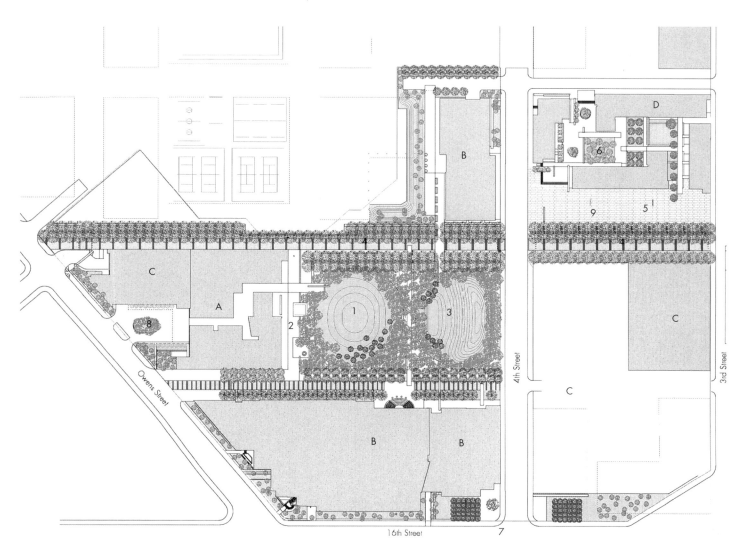

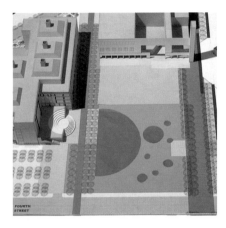

top
Workshop meetings

middle
Early models and sketches

bottom
Large presentation models

top
Laying stone
Stone benches

middle
Laying pavers
Paving patterns
Custom pavers

bottom
Rolling out turf
Decomposed-granite path
Amphitheater

University of California, Merced
Merced, California

Existing site with canal

154 In 1998 the University of California Board of Regents approved the construction of a new University of California campus to be built on a 2,000-acre agricultural site in the lower foothills of Merced. PWP was the landscape architect within a large interdisciplinary team led by Skidmore, Owings & Merrill (SOM) and BMS Design Group and including Fernau & Hartman Architects. Over the next few years the team produced a master plan and a long-range development plan. Then an infrastructure team was selected, led by Ove Arup & Partners, to prepare the first phase of the campus. SOM, EHDD, and Thomas Hacker Architects were selected as the first three architects to design the library, classroom, and science buildings respectively. PWP was retained to design the overall site landscape for the 110-acre first phase, details of which will become the guidelines for future campus landscape and site development.

Because of temporary ecological restraints, the first phase established by the master plan had to be constructed entirely within an irregularly shaped site on the extreme southwest corner of the future campus. Other complications include temporary entrance roads to the campus as well as difficulties with timing and initial funding availability. (Within the University of California system, all housing, parking, and recreation facilities must be supported directly by each individual campus rather than funded by the State.)

PWP was particularly aware that site standards and details would be extended into future phases; as a result each application needed to be developed with the future in mind. Site planning, long- and short-range development strategies, and first-phase construction had to be coordinated and synchronized. A seemingly "complete" initial campus had to be created in spite of the transient, partial, and complex process.

In addition to mass grading and engineering infrastructure, first-phase site development includes the initial campus entrance, entry and service roads as well as roads for second-phase construction, Library Plaza, Campus Green, the first of several automobile and pedestrian bridges, Main Street, ADA access, service for campus buildings, initial street-tree planting, canal planting, lighting, the first housing blocks, and the Wellness and Physical Education Center.

The formal entrance to the Merced phase-one campus is a semicircular drive lined with London plane trees and leading from an information kiosk down University Drive, also lined with plane trees. Pedestrians are separated from the parking lots and the initial housing construction by *Rhaphiolepis indica* hedges; bike lanes are curbside. At the turn of the entry road the hedgerow opens to a view that will eventually include a lake and student housing with playfields beyond.

The new bridge leads to the redwood-framed drop-off and turnaround directly in front of the library. The entrance to the chancellor's parking is just to the left. Shuttle buses from the entrance parking lots drop off here. The Entry Plaza (with a special palm garden display) adjoins Library Plaza and forms the beginning of Main Street, the major pedestrian spine of the campus, which is distinguished by custom-designed concrete unit paving and lined with circular seat planters, each containing four golden raintrees. Three steps join the building arcades to Main Street. Gentle ramps provide ADA access.

To the south is Campus Green, a formal grassed bowl with crossing paths spread out beneath a grove of canopy trees. Along the first section of the canal edge and also south of the bridge extends a plantation of waterside trees. A curving pedestrian path threads through both sides of the waterside planting.

The first phase will be completed in late 2005.

Master landscape plan

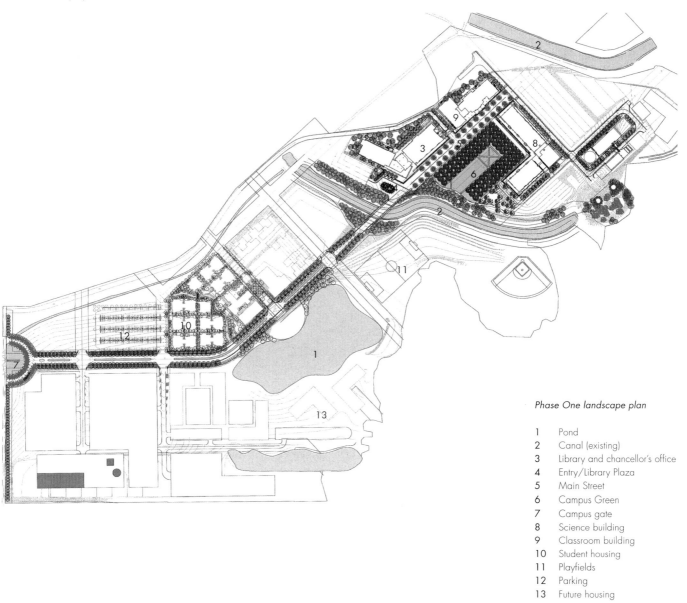

Phase One landscape plan

1   Pond
2   Canal (existing)
3   Library and chancellor's office
4   Entry/Library Plaza
5   Main Street
6   Campus Green
7   Campus gate
8   Science building
9   Classroom building
10   Student housing
11   Playfields
12   Parking
13   Future housing

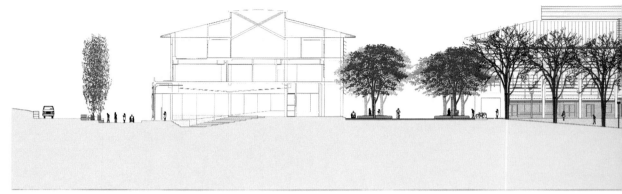

Section through Main Street and Campus Green

Section through University Drive, canal and bridge, Entry Plaza, and Main Street

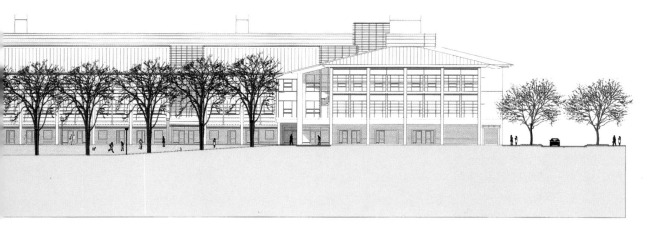

Campus Green

159

Federal Courthouse
Seattle, Washington

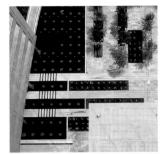

Entry fountain from above

PWP was part of a team with NBBJ Architects chosen to design the new federal courthouse in the Westlake district of downtown Seattle. The City hopes that the courthouse will spur private redevelopment of the surrounding blocks.

The 2.5-acre site slopes twenty-one feet diagonally from east to west. A plaza with a major fountain faces out to the corner of Stewart Street and Seventh Avenue as the main welcoming entry area. A grand stair joins the plaza with the lobby of the courthouse. Instead of a typical hard-paved Southern European courtyard, the plaza is in keeping with the moist, green atmosphere that distinguishes the region. Bands of metallic-quartzite pavement alternate with linear groves of birch trees, both bands running perpendicular to the stair and lobby. Beneath the trees lies a softer paving of irregular stone in a field of grass.

The plaza, which is furnished with benches, features a coffee stand with an informal outdoor café. A cascading fountain steps down the east side of the plaza parallel to the alternating stone and tree bands. It is planted with ferns and flowering water lilies. Behind the fountain a ramp provides ADA accessibility. In the heart of the plaza a sunken seating court features a commissioned work by artist Ming Fay.

The great entry stair bends around the building's corner in cascading steps and grass terraces that provide casual outdoor seating separated from the building's cafeteria by an intimate terrace planted with Japanese maples. Today security is a major factor in the design of all public buildings. In this case, the steep great stair protects the glazed lobby. Hardened tree supports alternating with wide circular precast-concrete seat bollards produce a defensible outer edge. Although seemingly open and inviting, the lobby and glass walls of the building are therby protected from an explosive vehicular attack.

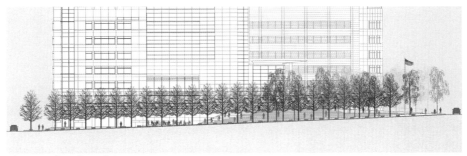

Elevation along Seventh Avenue

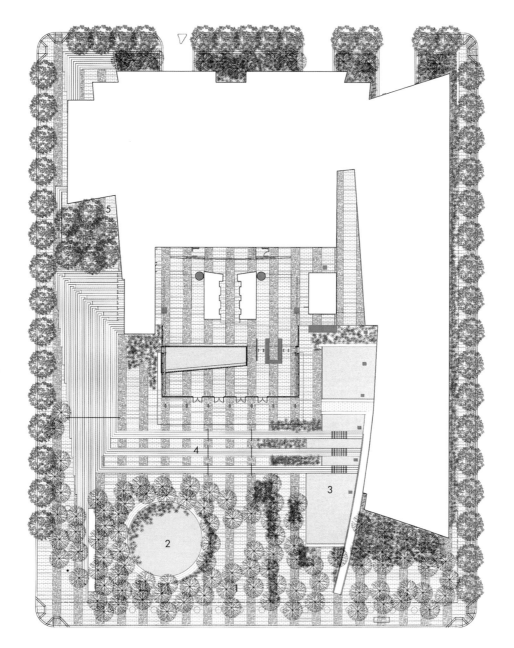

Landscape plan   161

1   Birch plaza
2   Sitting green
3   Stepped pool
4   Courthouse steps
5   Café

World Trade Center Memorial:
"Reflecting Absence"
New York, New York

Ground Zero

162

In November 2003 architect Michael Arad learned that his proposal for the World Trade Center Memorial was among the eight finalists selected by the WTC Memorial jury. Through a series of meetings with the jury he was encouraged to rethink the park level of the memorial and to collaborate on this development with a landscape architect. Arad selected Peter Walker and Partners. Over the next several weeks the park was developed under review of the WTC Memorial jury, and on January 5, 2004, the revised scheme was selected as the winner.

The concept of the proposal contains two gigantic voids representing the destroyed twin towers. These 200-by-200-foot voids, cut thirty feet into the site, are lined with water cascades that fall into a pool below and then disappear into a deeper, smaller void. The scale of the voids recalls the terrible losses of September 11, 2001. Ramped passageways lead the visitor down through darkness to the level of the pool, which is again visible through the cascade. Between the pool and the visitor stands a low parapet randomly inscribed with the names of the victims of the 1993 and 2001 terrorist attacks.

Below the north pool a chamber honors the victims whose remains could not be identified. The room is open to the sky. Adjacent to the chamber a museum displays artifacts of the World Trade Center destruction.

The memorial park is being designed to accomplish four main objectives:

First, to deepen and enlarge the visitor's perception of the level plane into which the voids are cut.

Second, to participate in the procession that is essential to the visitor's experience of the memorial.

Third, to separate the reverential mood of the memorial from the busy life of the surrounding city streets.

Fourth, to provide a quiet, beautiful, and human-scaled public open space for Lower Manhattan.

To accomplish these goals on a relatively small and irregular site, an abstract forest of dozens of deciduous trees with elongated trunks will be planted irregularly along a series of east-west lines, which Arad has likened to an abacus.

This scheme establishes an ordering system from the inside of the park rather than at its edges. From the north and south a visitor will experience what seems to be a naturalistic forest. From the east and west the visitor will experience the lines of trees as a series of colonnades.

Above the limbed-up trunks a canopy of leaves will provide a green rebirth in spring, welcome shade through the heat of the summer, and seasonal color in the fall. In the winter the sun will shine through a light tracery of bare branches. Through the trunks of the trees the flat plane of the park is visible in its entirety. The density of the trunks extends the apparent depth and size of the plane and at the same time softens the view of the immense buildings and the street life beyond. The trees stop before the voids, reinforcing the aspect of emptiness and loss.

The floor of the park will be made of elongated pieces of stone (eight by thirty inches) and low plantations of grasses, mosses, and flowering ground covers. At points of entry to the park and the memorial and in the areas surrounding the voids, the paving will be almost entirely stone, providing smooth, safe, comfortable walking surfaces. Beyond the heavily trafficked areas, the stone paving will gradually open up, giving way to predominantly planted surfaces, soft to the eye and to the touch. The design provides many benches for the memorial visitors as well as people from the neighborhood. A small clearing in the grove creates a space for family gatherings. By reminding the visitor of the natural cycle of life, the park will add a dimension of hope to the memorial.

right
Rendering of memorial and church park

Within the fountain

The Sacred Room

Ramp to the fountain

164   *Landscape plan*

1   North pool
2   South pool
3   Cultural buildings
4   Memorial forest
5   World Financial Center
6   Freedom Tower
7   Train station
8   St. Nicholas church

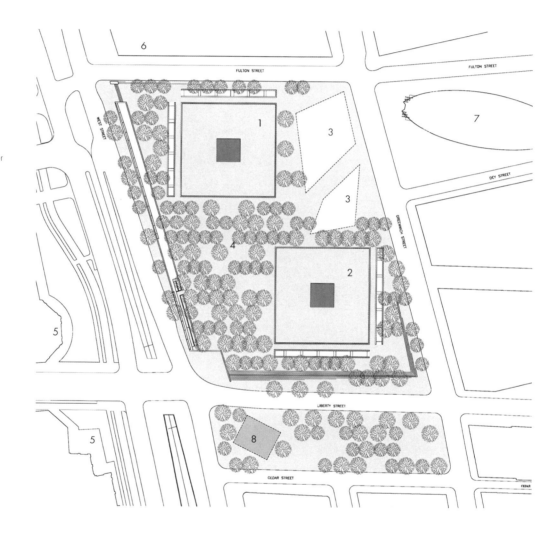

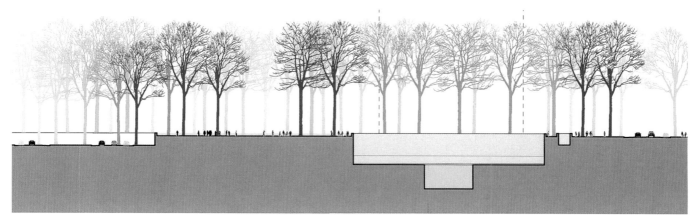

East-west section

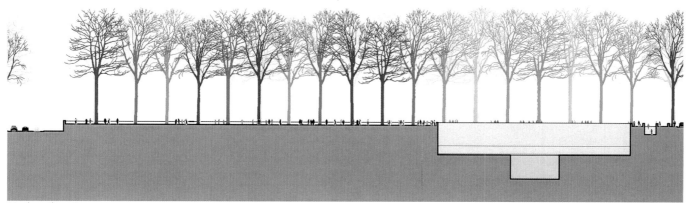

North-south section

pages 166-167
Rendering from Liberty Street

PLANNING AND URBAN DESIGN

ALTHOUGH MUCH MODERN ARCH-
ITECTURE CANNOT, OR DOES NOT,
DEAL WITH CONTEXT, ONE OF THE
MAJOR CONCERNS OF MODERN
LANDSCAPE ARCHITECTURE IS THE RE-
LATIONSHIP OF A SPECIFIC BUILDING
PROJECT TO ITS SURROUNDINGS. THIS
CONCERN IS OFTEN DIFFICULT TO PUR-
SUE IN PRACTICE BECAUSE LAND-
SCAPE BUDGETS AND PROGRAMS
TOO OFTEN RADIATE OUT FROM THE
MORE EXPENSIVE AND SPECIFICALLY
FUNCTIONAL NATURE OF THE BUILD-
ING. PRIOR TO 1929, LANDSCAPE AR-
CHITECTURE INCLUDED PLANNING
AND WAS BASED ON THE PARTICULARI-
TIES OF THE SITE AND THE LARGER
LANDSCAPE. PWP STILL APPROACHES
ITS COMMISSIONS IN THIS INTE-
GRATED MANNER.

Asahikawa Riverfront
Asahikawa, Japan

Asahikawa is the second-largest city on the island of Hokkaido, Japan. The city fronts on the Chu-Betsu River, and as in many older industrial cities, a large rail yard lies between the city and the river. The north-south grid of the city is perpendicular to the river, which floods to some degree each year, surrounding and occasionally inundating the rail yard and, more rarely, the downtown. The river is quite scenic, with large sandbars, meandering waterways, and picturesque stands of such water-associated trees as willow and cottonwood. The Japanese Corps of Engineers proposed channeling the river with steep concrete and stone embankments to control the flooding.

With the privatization of the Japanese national railway system, the City seized the opportunity to transform the abandoned downtown railroad yard. The master plan by Gen Kato of Nihon Toshi Sogo Kenkyu-shu, a distinguished Tokyo planning firm, and PWP resulted in a two-part urban park. To the west an enclosed lagoon, protected by the existing embankment and newly planted trees, allows such recreational activities as boating and swimming. To the east, the progression from city to river is articulated by an "ecological stairway" created by replacing the proposed Corps of Engineers' five-meter stone embankments with a series of broad terraced steps with lower stone walls

one meter in height. Each tier is planted with species of native riparian vegetation that would survive the predicted level of flooding. Thus, from the city down to the water, each descending tier is differentiated by species that thrive on an increasing degree of moisture and saturation. At the top are cultivated wet meadow grasses; in the middle, hardier sedges and reeds; and at the bottom, shrubs such as willow.

Since World War II, the city has grown along both sides of the river so that both parallel and cross-river vehicular transportation had to be increased. The plan proposed a new shoreline freeway above the flood levels and a series of bridges that would be high enough to span the river yet allow continuous pedestrian and bicycle traffic along its banks. Considerable attention was given to physical and visual connections between the streets and sidewalks of the existing downtown and the new development of the rail yard, the park, and the river. The city streets were to be extended as park allées.

Since many of the redevelopment parcels were complex in shape and topography, studies were made of each parcel to predict its holding capacity and economic yield, circulation for automobiles and service vehicles, and pedestrian access to the new parklands adjacent to and below the parcels.

The final plan was achieved through meetings and workshops that included the consultants, political and commercial leaders and their staffs, and the federal engineers and planners.

City plan

River and railroad yards

River view

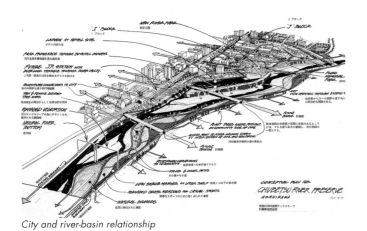

City and river-basin relationship

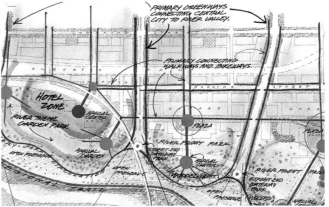

Pedestrian-circulation diagram of downtown to River Park

Park and wall development plan

1   Low walls
2   Pedestrian allées
3   Lagoon

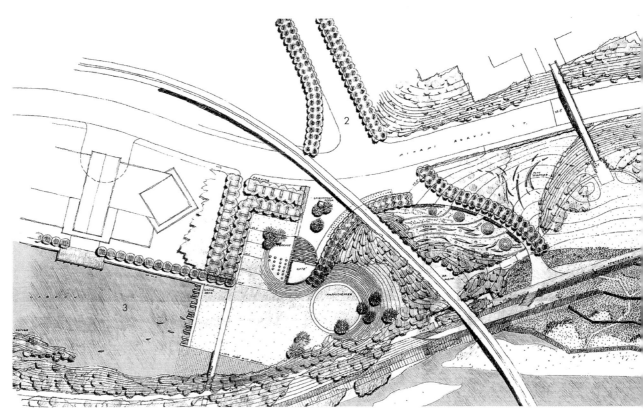

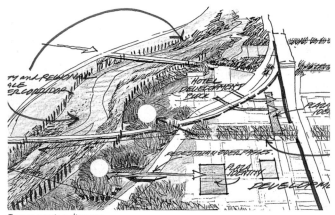

Transportation diagram

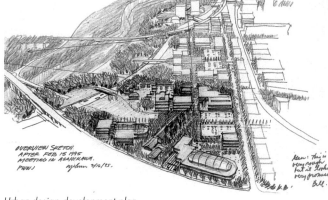

Urban-design development plan

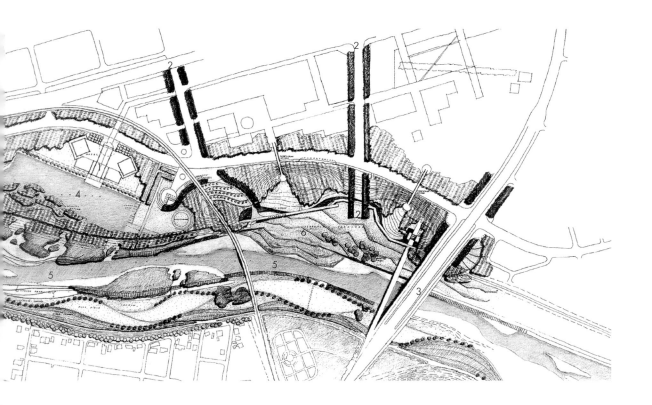

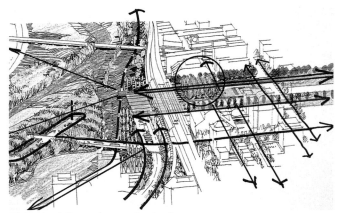

Major circulation and connection to city

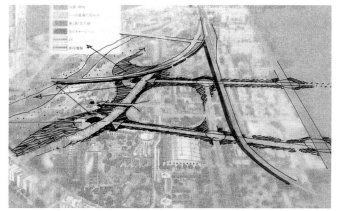

Three-dimensional bridge and freeway plan

River park and transportation plan

1   Downtown
2   Connecting allées
3   Major bridges
4   Lagoon
5   River and dune area
6   Park

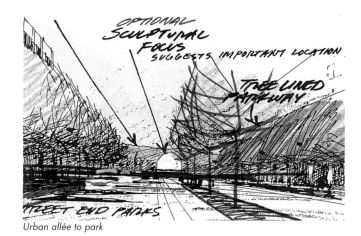

Urban allée to park

Street-side development

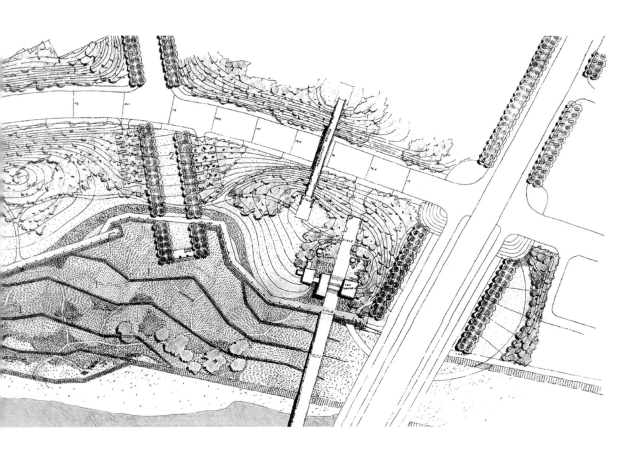

top
Lower water edge with dunes
Upper park with civic fountain

middle
Stepped ecological park
Middle park with flood-
resistant grasses

bottom
Upper park in summer
and in winter

Chiron Life Sciences Center
Emeryville, California

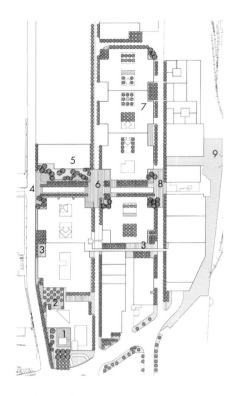

Chiron, a biochemical research company, was founded in a remodeled industrial building in the brownfields of Emeryville, California. Over the years, as the company grew, it acquired adjacent buildings and spread out to leased space throughout the city. In 1993, having acquired or optioned a number of additional sites adjacent to the original buildings, the founders—Bill Rutter and Ed Penhoet—hired Legorreta Arquitectos and PWP to prepare a master plan for consolidation and expansion. In addition to a land-use or development plan, they wanted a design vision for the architecture and open space of the new campus.

These ambitions posed problems for the City, which was only equipped to review land-use plans and proposals on a building-by-building basis. In order to review the proposal, the largest in its modern history, the City hired ROMA, an urban-design firm in San Francisco, to act as its consultant for urban-design review. What the architect and landscape architect produced was a three-dimensional vision that clearly represented Chiron's intent and elevated the public debate to specific questions of magnitude, scale, building, and open-space character that would probably not have emerged through the normal planning process. The company embraced this extended and costly procedure in order to accomplish its goals. Along with the usual issues of traffic, parking, jobs, and taxes, there were public debates about specific materials and color; architectural style; shadow patterns; public, semipublic, and private open space; and overall character.

Through an extensive series of workshops, neighborhood meetings, staff reviews, and public hearings came a gradual acceptance of the endeavor. The height of a single tower and the character of public and semipublic open space were the final hurdles for the plan. Animated studies of shadow patterns and an extensive set of open-space drawings and models gained public understanding and acceptance of the urban design, and a detailed development agreement was finally signed.

The first building includes a semipublic corner plaza with sculpture by Stephen de Staebler, a public park, a private interior courtyard, a roof garden, and the first of a series of semipublic street-front courtyards. The second building and a small linear park are now being designed. Public opinion indicates that the reality has met the hopes generated by this remarkable public process.

Landscape plan

1   Corporate arrival entry
2   Outdoor dining terrace
3   Public park
4   Hollis Street entry plaza
5   Temescal Creek "daylighting"
6   Chiron Plaza
7   Private gardens at upper levels
8   Horton Street entry plaza
9   Horton Street Landing park
     and bridge to Bay Street development

left
Preliminary urban design sketches

middle
Study models of public spaces

right
First phase of completion

Highbrook Business Park
Auckland, New Zealand

Aerial view of site

In 1997 the owners of the beautiful peninsula of Waiouru negotiated the building of a bridge that would connect the peninsula to New Zealand's main north-south freeway, reducing the drive to central Auckland from more than two hours to thirty minutes. PWP was asked to create a master plan that would transform the former horse farm into a development of office and light manufacturing with supporting commercial, retail, and professional uses for a worldwide corporate clientele. The task included the protection and use of the existing natural and cultural amenities.

The 477-acre peninsula juts out into Tamaki River and contains some 9.5 miles of scenic waterfront as well as half of an extinct volcano crater, which faces southwest toward the expressway and the new bridge. The existing hedgerows, wooden fences, and poplar windrows of the farm form a large grid overlaying the gently rolling ridgeline of the peninsula. Water views extend out north, south, and east from all levels of the site with important views to Mount Wellington to the northwest, as well as the distant skyline of downtown Auckland and its iconic Skytower. The manor house of the original owner sits on the edge of a small stream valley that has been developed over the years as a wind-protected exotic garden planted with the giant ferns and palms of New Zealand, many varieties of azaleas and rhododendron, and other flowering plants from the South Pacific region, China, and Europe.

An agreement with the City called for 150 acres of donated parkland (thirty-one percent of the total peninsula) and accommodation of the much-increased traffic required for access to the housing and commercial development beyond the site. In response, the crater was set aside for equestrian and park uses. It will be connected to a continuous shoreline linear park that includes a series of loops to the Crater Park for hiking, walking, cycling, and riding. The linear park opens up the entire water edge to the scenic advantage of both internal and through traffic.

The building sites—arranged on the grid lines generated from the sight lines to Mount Wellington and recalling the existing farm roads and paddocks—lie on the shelves of ancient beachheads rising from the shoreline road to the top of the ridge and afford every building a water view over the buildings below. Trees are placed at the sides of the sites—rather than on the streets where they would block views—producing windrows that step down the shelves parallel to the view lines to Mount Wellington.

Commercial retail uses, including food and service stores, are arranged along a ridgeline road with parking behind. Only short-term parking is allowed along the pedestrian-scaled streets. Professional offices are located above the shops and stores.

The original manor house and garden will serve as a public meeting room and small convention center. The new Highbrook Square, occupying a small prominence reaching out into the bay, will include a small hotel, the first services and shops, and a health club and gymnasium. Highbrook Square lies adjacent to the major intersection of the development, Highbrook Crossing, which provides an iconic vehicular entrance for the executive park and the linear pedestrian spine of the project. Planted boulevards, running parallel to the windrows, provide additional connections from the ridgeline road and the other developed streets. These boulevards are intended to extend and connect the linear-park uses and collect freshwater runoff for irrigation.

Except for Crater Park, the owner will install and maintain all public facilities, parks, and major native plantings, including hedgerows and roads. Many of the trees will be planted in time to achieve significant growth before the buildings are constructed. Special planting will visually connect the existing freeway and bridge to the parkway and developed office park.

View of site at grade

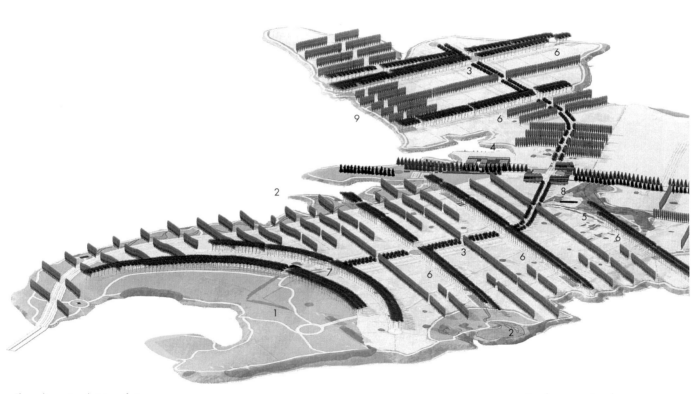

*Three-dimensional vision of site-
development master plan*

Landscape master plan

1 Pukekiwiriki Volcanic Crater Park
2 Southern esplanade
3 Main Street along the ridgeline
4 Highbrook Square and health club
5 Conference center
6 Park boulevards
7 Fig Grove Park
8 Highbrook Crossing
9 Northern esplanade

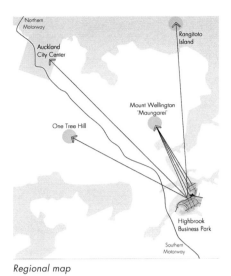

Regional map

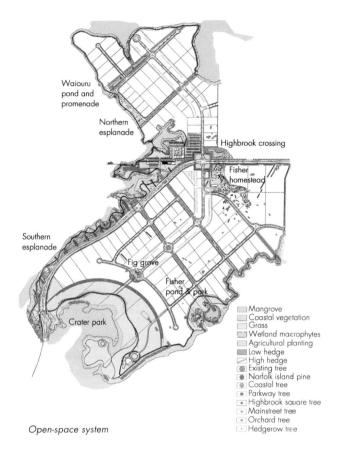

Open-space system

Mangrove
Coastal vegetation
Grass
Wetland macrophytes
Agricultural planting
Low hedge
High hedge
Existing tree
Norfolk island pine
Coastal tree
Parkway tree
Highbrook square tree
Mainstreet tree
Orchard tree
Hedgerow tree

Storm-water system

Overland flow catchment
Impermeable catchment
Treatment ponds

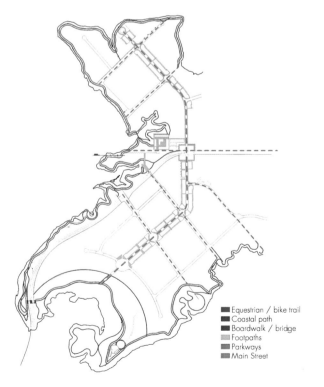

Pedestrian-circulation system

Equestrian / bike trail
Coastal path
Boardwalk / bridge
Footpaths
Parkways
Main Street

top
Pukekiwiriki Volcanic
Crater Park

bottom
Highbrook interchange
across the Tamiki River

178

top
Southern esplanade wetlands

bottom
Parkway planted with
Moreton Bay fig trees

179

top
*Hedgerows perpendicular
to Highbrook Drive*

bottom
*Main Street looking south
to Fig Grove Park*

Nishi Harima Science Garden City
Nishi Harima, Japan

Pine and oak forest with cryptomeria reforestation

Grading at beginning of plan

In 1990 architect Arata Isozaki, at the request of Governor Toshitami Kihara of Hyogo Prefecture, asked PWP to help prepare a long-range development plan for a new town then under construction on a 2,000-hectare site, 200 kilometers inland from Kobe, Japan, where a new supercollider —the largest in the world—was being constructed by the Japanese government. The town program included a new research university; a variety of housing for workers, scientists, and their families; a hotel and conference center; schools; areas for shopping and recreation; and a range of public-administration and service facilities.

The spectacularly beautiful site was mountainous, with steep volcanic hills wooded with oak and pine and a dense planting of *Cryptomeria japonica* that replaced the forest cut down in immediate postwar logging. Prior to PWP's participation, the development strategy was to grade off the tops of the hills and place the earth in giant fills in the valleys to produce expensive developable land that was bare and flat. The Japanese have long preferred to live on the level portions of the land—a preference stemming partly from the wealth that farmland has historically represented and partly from Japan's long history of earthquakes and landslides. Despite numerous modern examples of urban hillside development, these negative feelings persisted

in the prefecture staff and in the public at large. Furthermore, young professionals prefer to live in a culturally rich urban environment near family and friends. How, then, could an appealing environment be planned at Nishi Harima?

PWP set out to retain much of the natural environment, maximize the valley and mountain views, reduce extensive grading, and develop circulation and recreation systems that emphasized the beautiful natural conditions. The new plan first changed the flat lands along the access roads from commercial to cultural and recreational use, making them as visible as possible at the entrance to the town. Parks, playgrounds, children's play areas, concert halls, conference facilities, and the first elements of worker housing were organized into a highly visible and civic downtown. Most shopping was clustered in pedestrian-friendly complexes immediately visible from, but not lining, the roads. The existing golf course was visually opened up to emphasize a recreation-oriented lifestyle.

The master plan organized the required residential land into neighborhoods of single-family and multiple housing and schools connected by an integrated open-space system of small parks and preserved woods, continuous pedestrian greenways, bike paths, and a town-wide trail system. Roads were carefully fitted to the hillsides.

PWP led the prefecture staff in visits to various hillside developments both in Japan and California and produced a series of images that conveyed the character of the residential environment. Still, there was considerable resistance. After much difficulty, the firm asked Arata Isozaki for advice. He suggested that in order to address the cultural resistance PWP should put its argument and plans into a more persuasive form, and he asked a famous Japanese poet, Mutsuro Takahashi, to express the recommendations in elegant, highly poetic Japanese. With this explanation in hand, PWP presented the proposals to the governor, who thoughtfully reviewed the drawings and plans and then carefully read the arguments.

Although our office still does not know the exact contents of the poet's text, the governor was persuaded, and the plan was adopted. PWP prepared several illustrative neighborhood layouts and grading studies and reviewed the initial siting and open-space designs by other architects and landscape architects for the beginnings of the university complex, the initial retail and commercial development, the first city schools, and administrative and service facilities.

Pedestrian and bike paths through forested hills

Entry road through forest

Hillside living

Playfields

Open space system

Major vehicular circulation

Secondary vehicular circulation

Pedestrian circulation

Millennium Parklands
Sydney, Australia

Existing site, 1997

Millennium Parklands is made up of more than a thousand acres surrounding the site of the 2000 Sydney Olympics at Homebush Bay. The site is slightly larger than New York City's Central Park, but unlike Central Park or Golden Gate Park in San Francisco, it does not lie within an urban grid and, therefore, has no formal boundaries. Rather, various state, federal, and city parcels, including Bicentennial Park (recently built over a garbage landfill), have been cobbled together —hence the name "Parklands." These parcels may be extended over time, perhaps with additional lands across the Parramatta River and Homebush Bay.

Most of the Olympic and Parklands sites had been generally degraded, first by their use as an abattoir in the nineteenth century and then by chemical and heavy-manufacturing factories in the twentieth. More than sixty-five percent of the site was saturated to some degree with chemical waste, which had to be dug out before the site could be planted or used for recreational purposes. One of the historic stream basins had been totally filled with degraded soil, destroying its natural

flow and ecology. Specific legislation dictated that these toxic excavations could not be removed from the site. Additionally, a portion of the site was a storehouse for naval munitions, some of which are buried underground or possibly still present in the adjacent marshes. The Olympic site occupied most of the higher ground, leaving the lower and most degraded areas within the Parklands site.

Nevertheless, the Parklands site possessed some remarkable assets: more than fifteen miles of continuous waterfront along the Parramatta River and Homebush Bay; a naval base with a truly remarkable man-made landscape and a number of historic buildings, dating back more than a century; an almost unspoiled 124-acre aboriginal forest; substantial areas of mangrove swamp in the major inlets and river edge, some of which have been developed and maintained by Bicentennial Park as a nature preserve; bird sanctuaries in the mangrove stands; rare Golden Orb spiders; and Green and Golden Bell frogs, an endangered species. The Brick Pit is composed of some seventy acres of deep excavated layers of shale with a limestone quarry below. It is a reminder of the historic development of Sydney, a beautiful spatial feature of the site, and a major new habitat for the endangered frogs.

The park board and the Olympic Coordinating Authority (OCA) have envisioned a park for the twenty-first century that contrasts sharply with such nineteenth-century creations as Sydney's Centennial Park. The strategy for the development of the Parklands in the 1997 study breaks down into ten main tasks.

The first was to dig out the contaminated soil and place it in a series of positive landforms; some of these were small hills that were naturalistic in character, and some took the form of ziggurats, which are called markers. Spiraling paths lead to the tops of the markers, which range from twenty to sixty meters in height and serve as orientation monuments from various parts of the park while providing views over trees to the Olympic Center, the river and bay, and in the distance the skyscrapers of downtown Sydney. Since the earth caps of both sorts of landforms were thin, tree planting was kept to the deeper soil at their lower edges and shallow-rooted native grasses were sowed on the thin caps.

Early sketch plan of "walls and rooms" concept

Second, Haslam's Creek was completely restored into a seemingly naturalistic streambed leading down through the park to the Parramatta River. Designed pools on either side harvest the freshwater runoff for irrigation and naturally purify the water before discharge into the river. The whole area was replanted as a major riparian wetland with a variety of grasses, reeds, and submersible plants.

Third, the plan calls for an extensive linear reforestation around each of the parkland parcels in order to form continuous walls that separate each of the different functions of the park into great rooms. Within the forested walls, a system of separate linear paths— "green tubes" for walking, bicycling, and jogging—will connect all of the rooms in the park like hallways in a gigantic house.

Fourth, the surreal lawn of the naval base with its underground bunkers and the aboriginal forest area will be preserved with restoration of the historic naval buildings and repair and extension of a small electric train to provide visual access to the fragile forest and a popular ride for visitors of the park.

Fifth, the mangrove swamps will be permitted to reestablish themselves from Bicentennial Park all along the river, doubling the bird and insect habitat.

Sixth, a continuous lighted boardwalk and bicycle promenade will stretch the full length of the river and bay frontage. This promenade will be connected to the systems of park paths and biking trails.

Seventh, the Brick Pit will be preserved intact as a habitat and as a historical monument except for construction of safe access for small groups of school children and park visitors.

Eighth, the huge central surface-parking lot will be replanted and partially developed as a park arrival and service village that will provide information as well as the beginning point for train, jitney, bicycle, and pedestrian ways.

Ninth, the existing automobile boulevards will be replanted with additional forest walls and redesigned with a limited amount of short-term roadside parking for the convenience of picnicking families and disabled visitors.

Finally, the plan calls for the formation of a governing institute to help guide the development of the Parklands and its evolving program. Not unlike a small university, the institute will blend scientific nature study, cultural and natural history, and site-specific arts with scholar- and artist-in-residence programs, educational and outreach programs, and a program of exhibitions, festivals, and commemorations to expand the public activities of the annual Easter Show throughout the year. The institute will utilize the state-of-the-art information systems that were developed for the 2000 Olympics.

Most of the Parklands are designed to be dry and self-sustaining, although over time there can be a certain amount of green lawn for traditional park activities. Conventional athletic activities, such as tennis, golf, swimming, and organized field games, would make use of the existing Olympic facilities.

The plan has been adopted, and PWP is serving as continuing planning and design consultant to the park staff.

184

top
Endangered bullfrog
Mangrove swamp with pedestrian
boardwalks
Early railroad structure

middle
Early brick arcade
Munitions bunker
Aboriginal forest

bottom
Pier at naval base
Bunker with earth mounds
Parramatta River

Olympic center
Rebuilding
Preservation
Rebuilt water system

Marker
Excavation
Fill

Walls
Preservation
Grass

left
Parklands
Pedestrian and bicycle circulation

right
Excavation and fill
Planting and reforestation

Rebuilt Haslam's Creek with adjacent Olympic Village

Marker from Haslam's Creek

Restored mangrove wetlands

Rebuilt marshlands

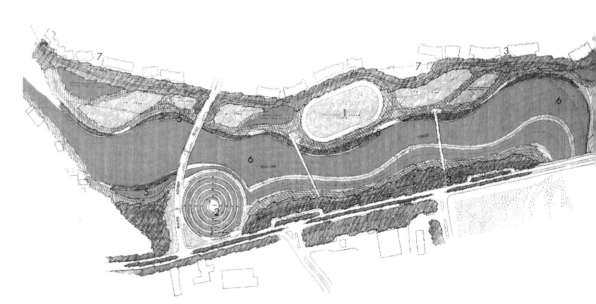

Reconstruction master plan of Haslam's Creek

1   Recreation
2   Marker
3   Reforestation "walls"
4   Freshwater ponds
5   Mangrove restoration
6   Restored waterway
7   Housing

Relocated wetlands

Playfields with sunflowers

Wetlands and marker

Water's edge boardwalk and bike trail

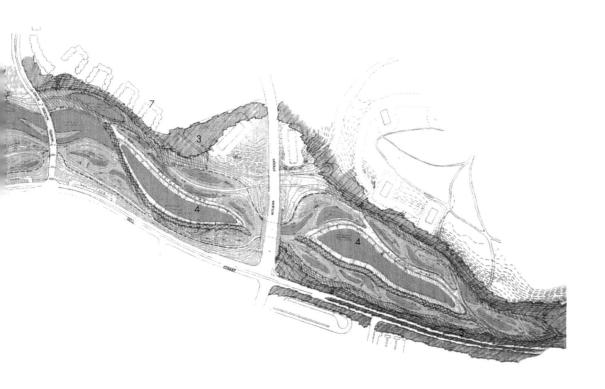

New Bay Bridge Waterfront Parks
San Francisco Bay, California

Aerial view

View of San Francisco Bay

Existing site at grade with cranes for the new bridge beyond

Regional diagram

In 1999, as part of the public debate over the plan to rebuild the antiquated cantilever section of the San Francisco Bay Bridge, PWP was asked to look at the marsh and wetlands restoration and recreation potential of the East Bay lands at the bridge entry. A number of the East Bay waterfront cities have begun to redevelop their once-industrial waterfront lands, for example, the Berkeley Marina and Cesar Chavez Park, the Berkeley Aquatic Park, the Emeryville Shoreline development between the Ashby Street and Powell Street off-ramps of the I-80 freeway, and the waterfront housing centered around the "Rosie the Riveter" memorial in Richmond. The success of these various developments depends in large part on their continuous linear pedestrian and bicycle connections;

hence, the importance of two major additional possibilities—the park uses of the West Oakland brownfield waterfront lands adjacent to the Bay and possible bicycle and pedestrian access to Yerba Buena and Treasure islands. In the future these routes might even extend a recreational connection to San Francisco by joining the new bridge section to a redesigned pathway along the remaining suspension section.

The introduction of bicycle and pedestrian pathways on the bridge is an economic, engineering, and finally a political issue, but the assumption that they might come about was the basis of PWP's studies and their urban-design images of the various possibilities for the new bridge and both sides of the existing highway waterfront.

Proposed waterfront marshland park

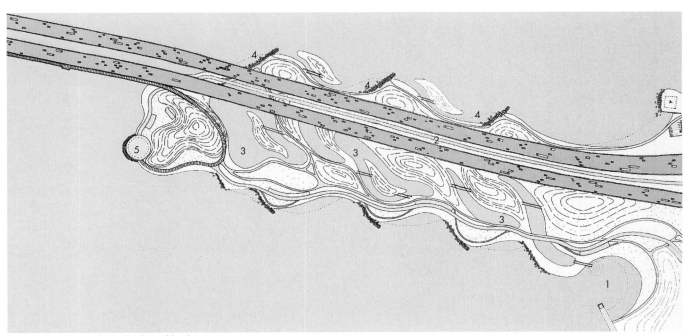

Proposed park on reclaimed industrial land

Landscape master plan

1 Lagoon
2 Bridge lanes
3 Wetland
4 Dunes
5 Lookout

Novartis Headquarters
Basel, Switzerland

Existing industrial site on Rhein River

In 1999 PWP won a competition to design the landscape of the Basel headquarters of pharmaceutical giant Novartis. The existing complex of mostly industrial buildings on a fifty-one-acre site beside the Rhein River lies halfway between the airport and the center of the city. The object of the competition was to transform a largely paved industrial landscape, crisscrossed with train tracks, into a modern research and administrative campus with a pedestrian-friendly ambience of trees, benches, greens, parks, and squares. In addition to the design of the open spaces, the landscape plan dealt with an extensive existing network of underground vaults and basements.

In 2001 Novartis commissioned Vittorio Magnago Lampugnani, the noted urban designer, planner, and teacher, to prepare a new urban-design plan for the campus development that would serve as a basis for a series of architectural competitions. The resulting plan called for an urban composition of mid-rise buildings in a grid of major and minor streets animated with greens, plazas, and pedestrian throughways. A large new park at the campus entrance would contrast with the intense urban grid of the buildings and set the stage for future public open-space development between Novartis and the river's edge.

The urban-design plan made a number of bold new proposals: a new entrance at Voltastrasse; the development of a campus spine along historic Fabrikstrasse; the removal of most cars from campus into a new parking structure and upgraded parking lots; and the future decentralization of restaurant and employee-service facilities into a new pedestrian arcade. Each segment of this arcade, which parallels Fabrikstrasse, would be produced through the coordinated design of the future buildings. Pedestrian-scaled, planted side streets would accommodate emergency fire and service functions. The plan calls for the scattering of additional restaurants and cafés as well as the development of a hierarchical series of open spaces, each with a distinctive character and all enriching the pedestrian orientation of the campus.

After the urban-design plan was adopted, Lampugnani assembled a committee to develop guidelines for the campus. The members include: Lampugnani, urban design; Peter Walker, landscape architecture; Alan Fletcher, graphic design; Andreas Schutz, lighting design; and Harald Szeemann, art acquisition. Continuing workshops assure that the guidelines address the many interrelated issues of campus growth such as the selection of street and plaza materials, wayfaring, street and open-space lighting, security and fire protection, pedestrian movement, public assembly, landscape accessibility, water expression, recreation, bicycle parking, and the acquisition and placement of major outdoor art. Through workshop submissions and review, an expanding set of specific guidelines was prepared and adopted by the company's campus steering committee, made up of the president, Dr. Daniel Vasella, his key division heads, the campus champion Wolfdietrich Schutz, and members of the design-workshop group. Within the overall direction of the urban-design plan, several of the architectural competitions have begun with attendant collaboration on landscape and art acquisition. The workshop team has been asked to remain during the first stages of development to work with company staff in realizing the urban-design and open-space development; to participate in the architectural juries; to help communicate the plan to employees; to integrate the design guidelines; and to act as a review, coordination, and screening agent for the president and the campus steering committee.

Proposed urban-design plan by
Vittorio Magnago Lampugnani,
Studio di Architettura

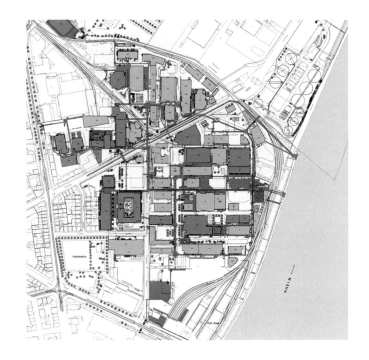

left
Plan of underground tunnel and vaults
Plan of service ways and short-term parking

right
Plan of main-entry and service access
Plan of bicycle-parking locations

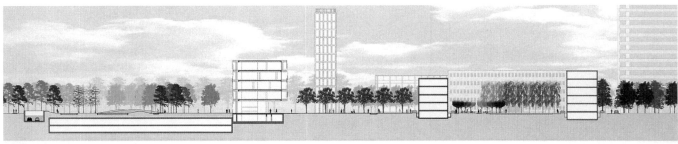

Section through parking garage with park above   *Forum*   *Headquarters courtyard*   *Green*

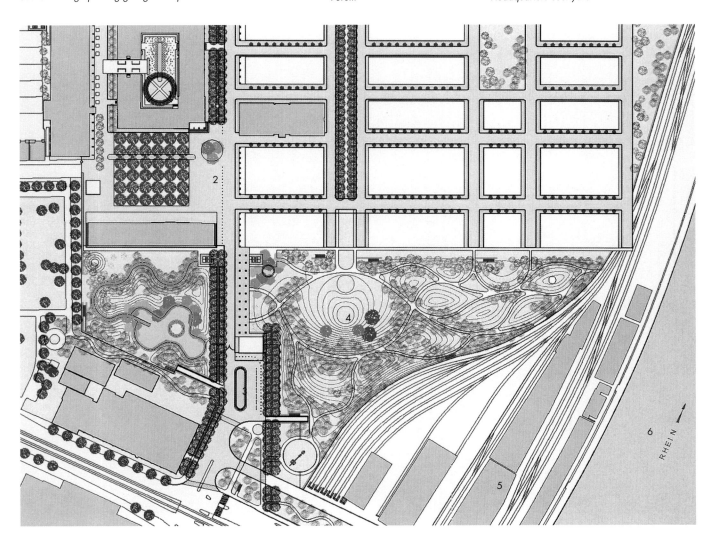

First Phase open-space development plan

1   Courtyard
2   Forum
3   Entry plaza
4   Park (above underground garage)
5   Port, future city park
6   Rhein River

Birch court in winter

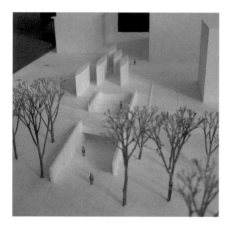

top
Novartis Forum
Sitting in the birch grove
Courtyard opening

middle
Northern pedestrian underpass
and Serra sculpture
Grass terrace
Shaded tables and chairs

bottom
Model of park over garage
The pool
Almost on axis

Left
Richard Serra sculpture

Plaza and underpass

Palo Alto Intermodal Transit Center
Palo Alto, California

Stanford entry, Palm Drive

University Avenue, Palo Alto

198

In 1992 Palo Alto and Stanford University initiated a planning study for the area between the entrance gates of the university at Palm Drive and the end of University Avenue, the main east-west street of the city. A committee made up of City leaders and staff, interested citizens, and the Stanford University planning staff acted as client.

From 1894 both the university and the city grew west and east away from the Southern Pacific train station. Students and citizens walked or rode in wagons or on horses in both directions. The Olmsted plan for the university initiated Palm Drive, which stretched from the station through the "arboretum" to the original quad. By the 1930s El Camino Real began to rival the railroad, and so an underpass was created for University Avenue underneath El Camino Real and the railroad tracks to speed up and encourage an increase in east-west traffic. This was one of the earliest grade separations in Northern California.

After World War II automobile traffic increased in volume and in speed, surpassing the railroad in volume as it served the low-density suburban housing that spread out into the countryside. In the late 1960s Palo Alto signalized University Avenue, reversing the policy of encouraging through traffic. Later, when the city redesigned University Avenue through the downtown to encourage and favor pedestrians, the vehicular logic of the underpass was obviated. In the past decades, El Camino Real has grown into a wide vehicular commercial street with increased signalization, leaving only the stretch of Stanford frontage as a through road. Palm Drive speed limits have also been reduced to twenty-five miles per hour.

The plan attempts to reorganize automobiles, buses, pedestrians, trains, and bicycles into a functioning physical system that would allow the space between Stanford and Palo Alto to become a recognizable and usable civic place.

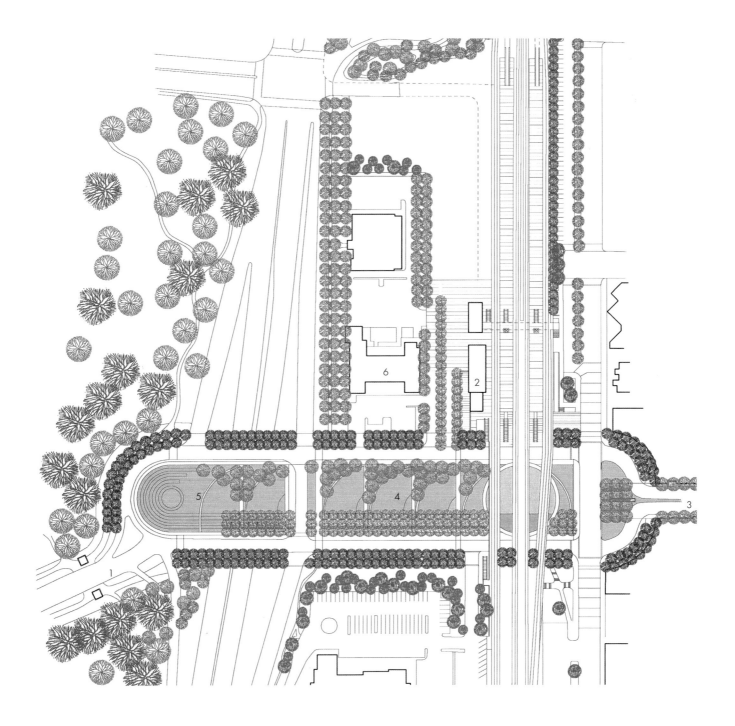

Urban-design plan

1   Stanford entry (Palm Drive)
2   Train station and underground
     bus station
3   Entrance to University Avenue
     (City of Palo Alto)
4   Park
5   Entry garden
6   MacArthur Park restaurant

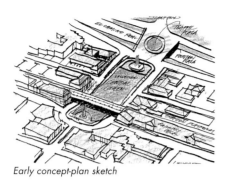

Early concept-plan sketch

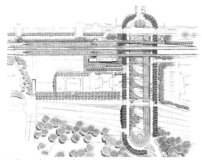

Urban-design plan

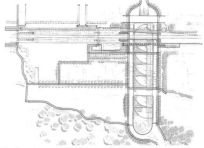

Pedestrian- and bike-circulation plan

MacArthur Park restaurant

Ramp to station plaza

Historic train station

*Historic ramp
with escalator*

*Southbound
Tracks*

*Section of Civic Park through pedestrian
underpass with the new transit center beyond*

The park

Tracks lined with poplar colonnade

Water feature terminating Palm Drive

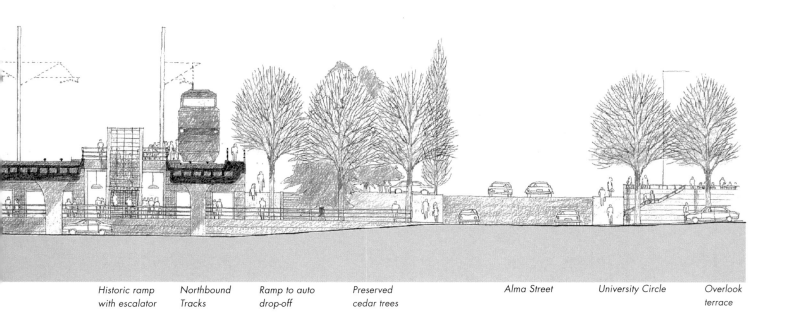

Historic ramp with escalator

Northbound Tracks

Ramp to auto drop-off

Preserved cedar trees

Alma Street

University Circle

Overlook terrace

Southwest Federal Center
Washington, D.C.

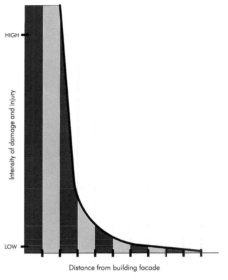

Blast damage danger

Unlike the ceremonial and monumental center of the nation's capital or the downtown commercial business center with its sprinkled federal presence, the Southwest district of Washington, D.C., is a dense concentration of federal offices built within the grid of District of Columbia streets. Strangely isolated from the grandeur of Pierre L'Enfant's Washington, with little existing open space and few amenities, it holds more than 70,000 daytime federal workers in public buildings as well as private facilities leased by the General Services Administration, which acts as landlord for the federal government. A raised railroad line that includes commuter services complicates the area, which is also served by everal Metro subway stations. The rail line uses—and disrupts—Maryland and Virginia avenues, two of the major diagonal streets oriented to the Capitol, both initiated by L'Enfant's plan. In addition, a major freeway separates the area from the Potomac River waterfront, and major arterial streets and limited-access ramps further divide the site.

Buildings in the Southwest district range from Federal Beaux Arts, dating from the 1930s, to a range of buildings in such modern styles as glass curtain wall, concrete brute, postmodern, and historicist, as well as quite ordinary commercial offices. The area includes: I.M. Pei's L'Enfant Center; Pei, Cobb, Freed's Holocaust Museum; and Marcel Breuer's HUD and Department of Education buildings.

The purpose of this study was twofold, with each goal of equal importance: increased safety, especially from terrorist intrusion and vehicular-carried explosives; and improved urban-designed streetscapes that would substantially upgrade the pedestrian and social environment.

This study, along with studies of the Mall area, Pennsylvania Avenue at the White House, and downtown Washington, D.C., provides the basis for construction proposals that are currently before Congress.

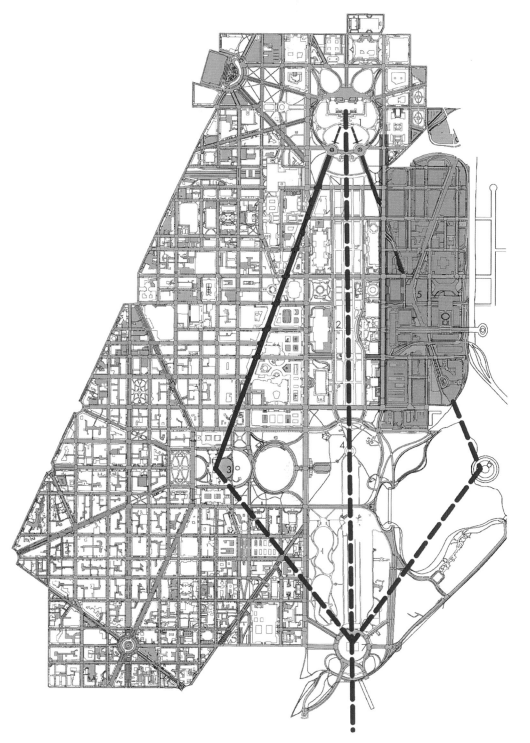

1   U.S. Capitol
2   Mall
3   White House
4   Washington Monument
5   Southwest Federal Center
6   Jefferson Memorial
7   Lincoln Memorial

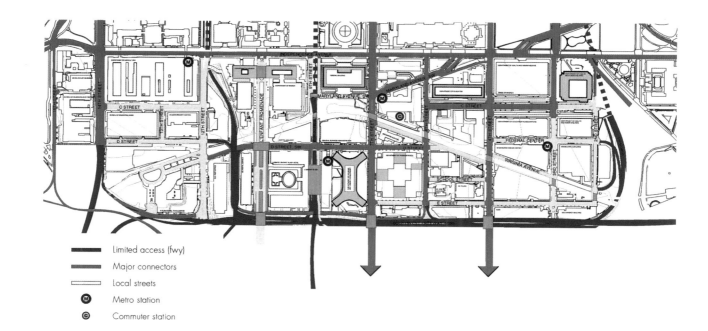

Limited access (fwy)

Major connectors

Local streets

Ⓜ Metro station

Ⓒ Commuter station

204

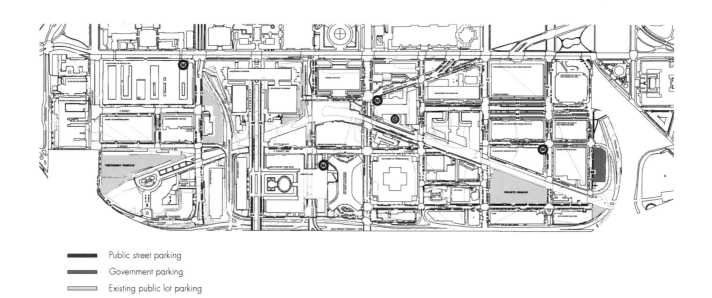

Public street parking

Government parking

Existing public lot parking

top
Circulation plan

bottom
Parking plan

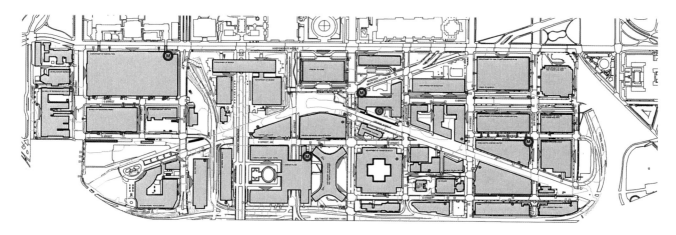

▲ Main entrances

▲ Emergency entrances

▲ Employee entrances

▲ Service entrances

▲ Parking entrances

● Guard entrances

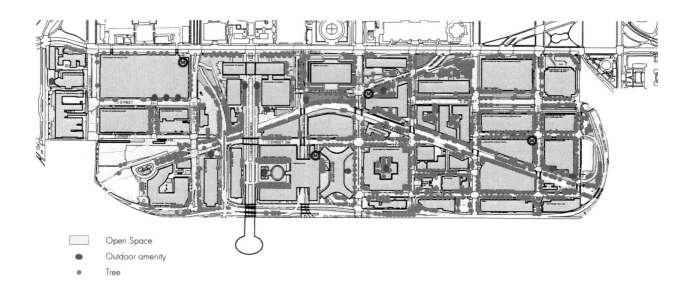

▢ Open Space

● Outdoor amenity

● Tree

top

Building-entrance plan

bottom

Open-space plan

206

top
View at HUD building

bottom
View at Maryland Avenue on axis
with Capitol

207

top
View along Fourth Street

bottom
View along Eye Street

Stanford University
Medical Center
Palo Alto, California

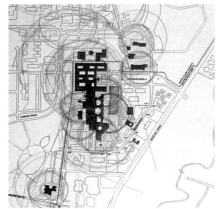

Pedestrian-zone diagram

Major-movement axis

208   Certain development areas are too dynamic to allow for a precise or fixed plan or even a rigidly standardized set of guidelines or procedures. Redeveloping downtowns, research campuses, and complex medical centers are but a few examples. Here the pieces and/or rate of development of buildings and such major infrastructure as roads, utilities, and open space are subject to unforeseeable events engendered by major new endowments, changing academic and administrative needs, and so forth. Such a problem area is the Stanford University Medical Center, which includes Stanford University Hospital, Children's Hospital, the Beckman Center, the Center for Clinical Science Research, the Clark Center, and various academic and research units, all with their less-than-predictable servicing, parking, and infrastructure needs.

Nevertheless, certain general requirements and relationships are foreseeable and, therefore, broad strategies can be instigated and smaller plans carried out. Over the past fifteen years, PWP, working with the campus planning staff, deans, and departmental chairs and committees, has provided the university with a series of plans and preliminary designs that project and test various possibilities as new needs emerge.

The plan for the Medical Center is in reality a continuing series of physical-planning studies that, over time, deal with opportunities and problems at many levels, all of considerable importance to the university, the faculty and staff, and finally to the architects of the individual buildings. These studies may result in major—and always evolving—functional and characterological changes to the campus. They are sometimes quite general and sometimes very precise, and they frequently involve alternative schemes. A small sampling of these plans and studies are included here. Each study is informed by background knowledge of overall campus development, and each aspires to improve incrementally the functional as well as the aesthetic quality of the Medical Center fabric and its open space.

Of general strategies that guide development, one important example in recent years has been the brainchild of Stanford campus architect and planner David Neuman. The concept is based on the insight that ubiquitous postwar surface-parking lots can be used as close-in building sites and as incremental financial support for new peripheral structured parking—a creative concept demanding careful implementation. For example, in 1990, a garage built parallel to an early addition to Stanford University Hospital blocked visual and pedestrian access to the north even though it was only three stories high. Larger garages have been built, and others are planned for the periphery of the campus, but at Pasteur Drive the traditional entrance to the Medical Center complex was deemed so important that a major parking structure planned for this visual axis was built underground at significantly greater expense. (See Stanford University Medical Center Parking Garage, pages 128-129.)

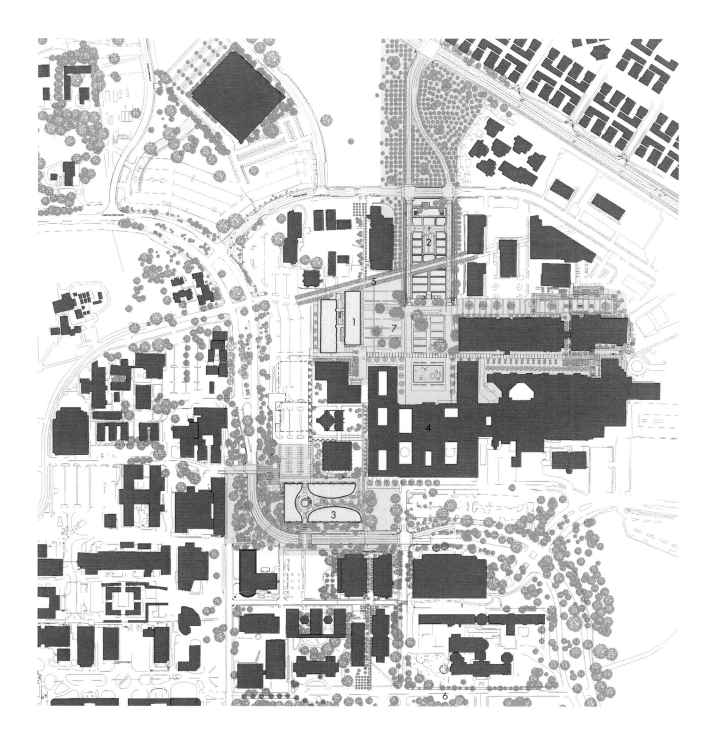

Current Medical Center campus plan

1   Center to Clinical Science Research
2   Underground garage
3   Clark Center
4   Stanford Hospital
5   Governor's Lane
6   Palm Drive
7   North garden

COMPETITIONS

WITH A FEW EXCEPTIONS, COMPETITIONS IN THE UNITED STATES SINCE WORLD WAR II HAVE BEEN A DISAPPOINTMENT FOR LANDSCAPE ARCHITECTS AND ARCHITECTS ALIKE. FEW WINNING DESIGNS ARE BUILT AND THOSE THAT ARE SELDOM LIVE UP TO EXPECTATIONS. EUROPE, HOWEVER, HAS A HISTORY OF NOT JUST BUILDING WINNING DESIGNS, BUT BUILDING THEM WITH THEIR CONCEPTUAL IDEAS INTACT. EUROPEAN COMPETITIONS HAVE SOUGHT AND REALIZED NEW DESIGN IDEAS AND HAVE FREQUENTLY PROVIDED THE KEY TO SUCCESS FOR YOUNG DESIGNERS. SOME EUROPEAN COMPETITIONS ARE FOR URBAN-DESIGN CONCEPTS FOR IMPORTANT CIVIC AREAS AND MONUMENTS. ESTABLISHED FIRMS ENTER THESE WITH NO HOPE OF SPECIFIC COMMISSIONS, SIMPLY AS A WAY OF SHARPENING THEIR IDEAS AND GETTING THEM OUT TO THE PUBLIC. AFTER FIFTEEN YEARS OF WORK IN EUROPE AND, MORE SPECIFICALLY, PARTICIPATION IN COMPETITIONS WITH MURPHY/JAHN AND FOSTER AND PARTNERS, PWP BEGAN TO ENTER COMPETITIONS ON OUR OWN IN EUROPE, ASIA, AND FINALLY THE UNITED STATES. THESE EXERCISES, WIN OR LOSE, ARE ENJOYABLE AND ENERGIZING TO THE OFFICE, AND WE FIND THAT THE CONCEPTUAL DEVELOPMENT IS OFTEN APPLICABLE TO FUTURE PROJECTS.

American Veterans Disabled for Life
Memorial: The Sacred Grove
Washington, D.C.

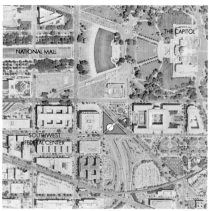

Aerial view

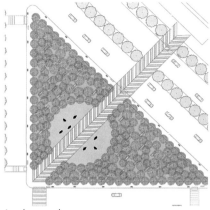

Landscape plan

212

Successful monuments require a sufficiently unique identity to remain in the memories of those who visit them as well as those who view a reproduced image. They also need to be rich enough in their design to sustain interest over multiple viewings. PWP's design for the memorial for disabled veterans is an example of this sort of complex requirement. The proposal combines simple elements (trees, paving, mist, sculpture, benches, light, and space) into a memorable and moving memorial that can exist alongside, but distinct from, the other designed spaces that physically define Washington, D.C., and, taken together, symbolically represent the history of the United States.

Approximately 200 cryptomeria trees are placed in a random configuration on triangular Parcel A. A thirty-foot-wide path cuts through the grove along a line of sight centered on the Capitol dome to the northeast. The path, of contrasting dark and light gray-green granite laid in a monumental chevron pattern, honors the military nature of the memorial.

A circular glade is carved into the center of the grove. On each side of the path, a half circle of bronze grill covers a below-grade concrete vault that has three purposes: to act as a manifold for a mist fountain, to collect surface drainage, and to contain the fountain lights. The fountain is an evenly maintained ten-inch layer of dry mist covering the entire area of the bronze grill and providing an ambiguous and mysterious base for the five to seven monumental bronze sculptures that form the centerpiece of the memorial.

The mist fountain is quite dry. Visitors can walk or wheel through it without getting wet. Since the mist is lighter than air, the slightest breeze carries it horizontally through the grove—a tactile experience for sighted and non-sighted alike, as is the fragrance of the trees. The mist, interacting with the sculptures and the trees, produces a subtle, but memorable image, both kinetic and mysterious. The mist fountain and sculptures are conceived as one piece. The sculptures, which vary in height from twelve to fifteen feet, will be the commissioned work of a single artist and represent the honored men and women in either a realistic or slightly abstracted style.

Visible from adjacent roads, paths, sidewalks, nearby parks and plazas, and from the freeway, the Sacred Grove contains twenty-eight wooden benches that are placed to provide views of the fountain and sculptures through the trees. The dimensions of the benches allow for the comfortable transfer from a wheelchair and can accommodate five or six people on each side. Each bench broadcasts a varied program of music and/or spoken words heard only when someone sits on the bench. Beneath the trees the ground is paved with a stabilized decomposed granite.

All surfaces of the memorial, including the fountain, are continuous and flat, allowing complete barrier-free movement in the universal design tradition.

Parcel B contains handicapped parking for twenty vehicles with a specially paved and marked barrier-free connection to the grove. Parcels B and C are planted with Saucer Magnolia (*Magnolia soulangeana*) and ground cover to contrast visually with the grove and to provide a visual and psychological barrier from the highway.

At night the mist fountain is lit from below with a soft, warm light that silhouettes and partially illuminates the sculptures. Pale blue up-lights from the benches dapple the trees of the grove and emphasize the complexity of their natural form and random placement. Light defines the path's edges and spills out from the sides of the benches to create a safe and welcoming atmosphere. The whole composition produces a memorable nighttime image without diminishing the dominance of the lighted Capitol dome.

*View through the Sacred Grove
to the Capitol dome*

Civic Plaza
Reno, Nevada

Proposed plaza plan

When PWP was invited to a limited competition to design a new civic plaza for Reno, Nevada, on the downtown banks of the Truckee River between Virginia and Center streets, the firm encountered a site that was cut off visually from the river. PWP recommended scooping out a portion of the land and building a semicircular stone and grass amphitheater that stepped down seven feet, opening up views to the river from the proposed plaza. PWP also suggested a large semicircular raised porch at the entry to the adjacent city hall and government building. Sight lines from the porch would also open to the river.

A continuous carpet of sand-molded brick paving would cover the plaza from the west side of Virginia Street to the east side of Center Street, reaching across two bridges and producing a new plaza on the north side of the historic post office from which a grand sitting stair would descend to the river's edge.

All curbs would be removed with automobile and pedestrian traffic separated by a system of stone bollards that would allow extension of the plaza by closing off one or more of the streets. Two semicircles of large deciduous trees would provide shade. Cafés would be located on the city hall porch and beneath the raised bandstand at the river's edge, and two restaurants were also suggested, one on the plaza and one on the first two floors of an adjacent garage. Overhangs of the plaza restaurant and the bandstand café would contain heat lamps to encourage outdoor café life even in the winter.

A grand civic fountain—gentle enough for small children's play—and an ice rink for outdoor winter use would be built into the amphitheater.

The plaza was intended to receive and support a large number of civic events and festivals, from art and vintage-car shows to theatrical and musical performances. Although directly adjacent to the raucus downtown gambling center, it was designed as a dignified expression of the civic purpose of the residents of Reno as well as a site of activities for citizens and visitors of all ages from around the world.

Landscape plan

1   Amphitheater
2   City hall porch and steps
3   Civic fountain
4   Post office steps
5   Civic lantern and café
6   Restaurant
7   Bollarded cross street
8   Grove

Existing site

left
Spring   Children playing in the fountain
Summer   Fourth of July celebration

right
Fall   Evening performance
Winter   Ice-skating

Tokyo Train Station
Tokyo, Japan

Zen garden

Mosaic paving

Detail

Each day thousands of travelers and commuters use Tokyo Train Station—the largest station in Japan. For years, taxi, bus, and limousine drop-off and pick-up have been located at the back side of the station in a large asphalt-paved space—part parking lot and part industrial service yard. A consortium of clients commissioned two new high-rise office buildings and an entrance canopy for this side of the station, leaving the historic Victorian façade and the gardens untouched. The new buildings accommodate all existing uses as well as the access and emergency egress from the shopping and service areas below.

Murphy/Jahn, Inc., the architects of the new buildings, designed an elegant glass canopy for the waiting and arrival space. City traffic engineers produced a layout plan that maximizes efficiency of all parking and vehicular movements but offers little in the way of elegance. PWP's proposal for the new plaza employs two bold but complementary graphic patterns: one for the pedestrian plaza level and entry, the other—on an area six inches lower—for vehicular movement and short-term parking. The pedestrian-plaza surface would be a complex circular pattern executed as a mosaic of small stone setts laid in contrasting bands of deep red and white. Circular clear-glass barriers of various heights would surround the required stairways, and circular translucent-glass walls would surround all vents. The design would include a variety of furnishings within the pattern of the paving.

The vehicular patterns would be composed of orthogonal stripes of large black and white granite cobbles that define the main taxi and bus-parking areas without further striping or indications. The cobbles would be appropriate for heavy vehicular use. The contrast between the forms, colors, materials, and scales of the two paved levels would increase the pedestrian's awareness of intended uses, thereby enhancing safety.

View of plaza

Pool and paving at new entry

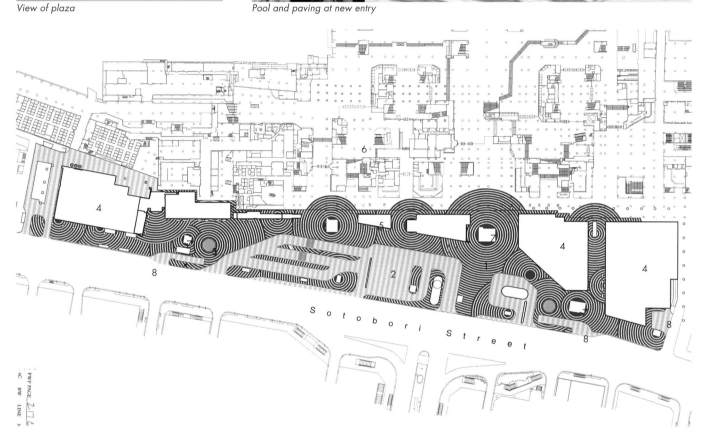

S o t o b o r i   S t r e e t

Landscape plan

1 Mosaic pedestrian plaza
2 Cobbled automotive areas
   (cars, taxis, buses, trucks)
3 Fountain
4 Office building
5 Entry building
6 Existing station
7 Stairway
8 Service entry

1600 Pennsylvania Avenue
Washington, D.C.

In a limited competition PWP proposed a redesign that would emphasize the pedestrian use of Pennsylvania Avenue as it runs in front of the White House at the edge of Lafayette Park. A series of minimal moves would accommodate all of the required vehicular and pedestrian functions while maintaining the spatial and visual importance of the street.

Pennsylvania Avenue is perhaps the most important street in America. It links the congressional branch of the government at the Capitol to the executive branch at the White House, formally, symbolically, and, once every four years, ceremonially. At 1600 Pennsylvania Avenue, the home of the President of the United States and one of the best-known addresses in the world, the White House commands a series of formal buildings and classical open spaces—the White House grounds, the Ellipse to the east, and Lafayette Park to the west. Citizens and visitors come to this spot to see the White House, to photograph it, to assemble in front of it in protest or support, and to visit the symbolic heart of power. In L'Enfant's 1796 plan, the principal avenues of the new capital city were named for the most important northern and southern states. In this proposal Pennsylvania Avenue carries unusual symbolic weight as the birthplace of a democracy that through the Constitution and its amendments ensures the right of assembly. A distinguishing stylistic correlative of this right is transparency of use; people in the United States enjoy, at the very least, visual access to the places of power. In the instance of Pennsylvania Avenue, then, the public street is an important symbolic component in every action that takes place at the White House.

Crude temporary security precautions have transformed some three blocks of what was once a heavily trafficked avenue into an impromptu walking street with access for only a few carefully screened vehicles, emergency fire and ambulance vehicles, and, in the future, a small bus called the Circulator.

In the PWP design, the security measures have been improved and made more discrete by integrating the guardhouses at either end of the avenue into the landscape in a less visible and less threatening form. Within Pennsylvania Avenue proper, two low circular fountains would continue the design of the existing White House fountain to unify the White House grounds with the street. The fountains would mark the axes of two of L'Enfant's principal diagonal streets, Connecticut Avenue and Vermont Avenue, which reach out into the city at the western edge of Lafayette Park. When turned off, the fountains would allow unrestricted pedestrian and vehicular activity.

Along Pennsylvania Avenue on either side of the fountains, ten circles (four composed of hedge and bench, six of hedge and flowers) would enliven the pavement. All the planting would be low so that the entire length of the avenue would be visually accessible to guards in the guardhouses and to pedestrians in the street. The changing floral expressions of these beds, some seven over the course of the year, would further integrate the area with the rest of Washington, D.C. Planting on Pennsylvania Avenue would extend existing formal programs of seasonal color, hedges, and trees along the edge of Lafayette Park and the White House garden. There would be no trees or permanent plants within the curb lines of Pennsylvania Avenue. All planted features could be taken up or disassembled for the inaugural celebration.

The spaces that make up the park, the avenue, and the grounds would be laid out along classical lines. PWP proposed a classically minimal strategy to join the various styles since they were created over a long period of time. All features in and at the edges of the avenue would reference both the White House garden and historic Lafayette Park and extend the scale and the importance of both so that they would participate in, rather than merely border, the avenue. Slightly narrower sidewalks would encourage pedestrian use of the avenue itself while emphasizing the north-south visual axis running through the center of Lafayette Park to the portico of the White House. Lights and two-way benches would edge the widened brick walkway at the southern edge of Lafayette Park. The wall at the base of the White House fence would be slightly modified to lift visitors to the grade of the White House lawn. All changes to President's Park would be simple and below eye-level, and they would leave the White House clearly visible to the rest of the world, which generally experiences this physical area through media images.

Paving materials would be limited to sand-formed brick sidewalks, large-scale granite street paving, and carved granite cuts—all long-lasting materials that require little maintenance. The retractable barriers at the ends of the avenues would be stainless steel and as fine in diameter as security requirements allow. Pedestrians would read them in the manner of the guardhouses, as simple, transparent, and unthreatening.

All barriers, including the guardhouses, could be removed for Inauguration Day. In the future, when security is no longer an overriding issue, the changes initiated by this design could be easily removed and the street returned to its original functions and the full strength of its symbolic potency.

Section through Lafayette Park, Pennsylvania Avenue, and the White House

Park

Promenade

Renwick Gallery at Seventeenth
Street entrance

View toward Jackson Place

View toward Executive Park entrance

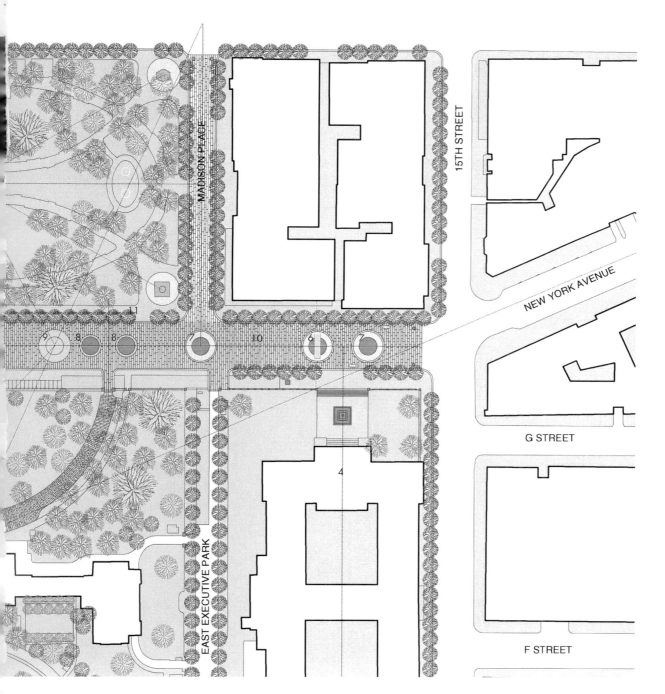

Landscape master plan

1   White House
2   Lafayette Park
3   Old Executive
      Office Building
4   Treasury Building
5   Renwick Gallery
6   Control booth
7   Temporary hedge
      and flower planter
8   Temporary hedge
      and bench planter
9   Pool
10   Stone paving
11   Brick paving

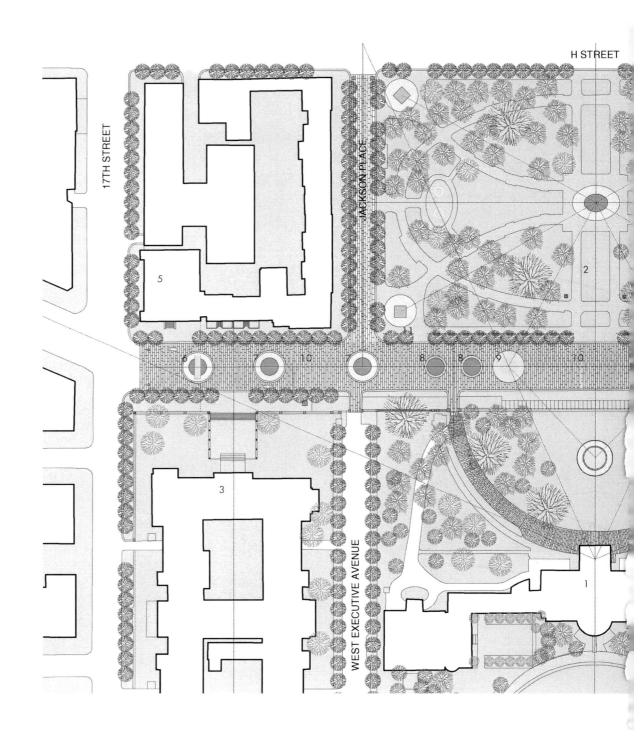

H STREET

17TH STREET

JACKSON PLACE

WEST EXECUTIVE AVENUE

5

2

11

9   10   8   8   9   10

3

1

Fountain

White House lawn

*White House from Lafayette Park
across Pennsylvania Avenue*

010481680

*Proposed stone paving and
fountain from the new promenade
at Lafayette Park*

CREDITS

PETER WALKER AND PARTNERS WOULD LIKE TO EXPRESS SPECIAL APPRECIATION TO THOSE WHOSE WORK OVER THE PAST TWO YEARS HAS MADE THIS BOOK POSSIBLE: DAVID WALKER, JAMES A. LORD, KELLY SPOKUS, TAYA RHODES, TIM WIGHT, CHRISTIAN WERTHMANN, SARAH KUEHL, JEFF ULM, SANDY HARRIS, JANE WILLIAMSON, APRIL DEERR, AND CHRIS VARESI, ALL FROM OUR STAFF; JOHN BELA, MEGAN GRISCOM, JOHANNA PHELPS, MAURA ROCKCASTLE, AND WAN-CHIH YIN, INTERNS FROM SUMMER 2003; GINA CRANDELL AND SUSAN PENNACCHINI.

Project Teams

American Embassy
Beijing, China
Page 140
Client: U.S. Department of State
Architect: Skidmore, Owings & Merrill

Asahikawa Riverfront
Asahikawa, Japan
Page 170
Client: City of Asahikawa
Architect: Gen Kato
Urban design: NTSK
River engineering: Hokkaido Engineering
Consultants

Bangkok Airport
Bangkok, Thailand
Page 144
Client: Airport Authority of Thailand
Architect: MJTA Consortium (Murphy/Jahn,
Inc., TAMS Consultants, and Act Group
Building)

Bayer Headquarters
Leverkusen, Germany
Page 76
Client: Bayer Pharmaceuticals
Architect: Murphy/Jahn, Inc.

Chiron Life Sciences Center
Emeryville, California
Page 172
Client: Chiron Corporation
Architect: Legoretta Architectos
Architect of record: Flad and Associates
Consultant for urban-design review: ROMA
Artist: Stephen de Staebler

Civic Park at Martin Luther King Jr. Promenade
San Diego, California
Page 70
Client: Center City Development Corporation
Artists: Andrea Blum and Dennis Adams
Engineers: Church Engineering
Urban designer: Austin Design Group

Clark Center for Biomedical Engineering and Sciences
Palo Alto, California
Page 124
Client: Stanford University
Architect: Foster and Partners
Architect of record: MBT Architectects

Copia: The American Center for Wine, Food, and Arts
Napa, California
Page 114
Client: Copia
Architect: James Steward Polshek

Deutsche Post Headquarters
Bonn, Germany
Page 148
Client: Deutsche Post
Architect: Murphy/Jahn, Inc.

Federal Courthouse
Seattle, Washington
Page 160
Client: General Services Administration
Architect: NBBJ Architects

Highbrook Business Park
Auckland, New Zealand
Page 174
Client: Noel Robinson,
Highbrook Development Ltd.
Investment and development management:
Innovus (Richard Stilwell and Steve Martin)
and McConnell International Property Ltd.
Engineers: Peter Yendell, GHD
Architect: Patrick Clifford, Architectus

McConnell Foundation
Redding, California
Page 60
Client: The McConnell Foundation
Architect: NBBJ Architects

Millennium Parklands
Sydney, Australia
Page 182
Client: Sydney Olympic Park Authority
(Brian Newman, chief executive officer and
director; David Grant, executive director and
executive director of Parklands place making;
David Young, executive director and
executive director of place management;
Jim Stone, director of capital works; Barbara
Shaffer, project manager of Parklands;
Charlotte Gay, urban design coordinator)
Olympic Coordination Authority (Peter
Duncan, director of Millennium Parklands,
and Dianne Leeson, director of planning
and urban design)
Collaborating landscape architects: Tony
McCormick, HASSELL, Bruce McKensie
Design
Engineers: Kinhill Engineers
Recreation: HM Leisure Planning
Lighting: Barry Webb and Associates
Landfill engineers: R.H. Amaral and
Associates

Nasher Foundation Sculpture Center
Dallas, Texas
Page 130
Client: The Nasher Foundation
Architect: Renzo Piano Building Workshop
Architect of record: Beck Architecture

New Bay Bridge Waterfront Parks
San Francisco Bay, California
Page 188
Client: Cal Trans

Nishi Harima Science Garden City
Nishi Harima, Japan
Page 180
Client: Hyogo Prefectural Government and
the Public Enterprise Agency
Architect: Arata Isozaki and Associates
Collaborating landscape architect: HEADS Co.
Lighting: Lighting Planners Associates
Street furnishings and signage: G.K. Sekkei
Associates

222

223

Selected Honors, Awards, and Competitions

2004   First Place, Design Competition for World Trade Center Memorial, New York, New York; architect, Michael Arad

ASLA Honor Award (Design): Nasher Foundation Sculpture Center, Dallas, Texas; client, Nasher Foundation; architect, Renzo Piano Building Workshop

ASLA Merit Award (Design): Copia: The American Center for Wine, Food, and Arts, Napa, California; client, Copia; architect, James Steward Polshek

ASLA Merit Award (Design): Saitama Plaza, Saitama, Japan; client, Saitama Prefectural Government; design team, PWP, OHTORI Consultants, NTT UD Architects

Illinois Landscape Contractors Association, Gold Award, Excellence in Landscape: UBS Tower (One North Wacker), Chicago, Illinois; client, John Buck Company; architect, Lohan Caprile Goettsch Associates; contractor, Walsh Landscape Construction

2003   ASLA Honor Award (Planning): Highbrook Business Park, Auckland, New Zealand; client, Highbrook Development Limited and Innovus

2002   ASLA Merit Award Oregon Chapter (Design): Jamison Square, Portland, Oregon; client, Portland Parks and Recreation and Portland Development Commission

2001   Developer of the Year Award for 2001 (Planning): Portland Parks, Portland, Oregon; client, Portland Parks and Recreation and Portland Development Commission

2000   First Place, Design Competition for Churchill Place, Canary Wharf, London, England; architect, Gensler

1999   First Place, Site Planning Competition for Novartis St. Johann Campus, Basel, Switzerland; architect, Gensler Associates

1998   Redding Urban Design Award: The McConnell Foundation, Redding, California; client, The McConnell Foundation; architect, NBBJ Architects

ASLA Classic Award: Weyerhaeuser Corporate Headquarters, Tacoma, Washington; client, Weyerhaeuser Company; architect, Skidmore, Owings & Merrill

ASLA Honor Award (Planning): Asahikawa Riverfront, Hokkaido, Japan; client, City of Asahikawa; architect, Gen Kato, NTSK

ASLA Honor Award (Design): Library Walk, University of California at San Diego; client, University of California at San Diego

ASLA Honor Award (Design): The McConnell Foundation, Redding, California; client, The McConnell Foundation; architect, NBBJ Architects

ASLA Honor Award (Design): The Principal Financial Group, Des Moines, Iowa; client, The Principal Financial Group; architect, Murphy/Jahn, Inc.

ASLA Merit Award (Design): Center for Advanced Science and Technology, Hyogo Prefecture, Japan; client, Hyogo Prefecture Government and the Public Enterprise Agency; architects, Arata Isozaki and Associates; collaborator, HEADS Co.

ASLA Merit Award (Design): Hotel Kempinski, Munich Airport Center, Germany; client, Flughafen München GmbH; architect, Murphy/Jahn, Inc.

ASLA Merit Award (Design): Martin Luther King Jr. Promenade and Civic Park, San Diego, California; client, Center City Development Corporation; urban designer, Austin Design Group

1997   ASLA Honor Award (Design): Longacres Park, Renton Washington; client, The Boeing Company; architect, Skidmore, Owings & Merrill

ASLA Merit Award (Design): Toyota Municipal Museum of Art, Toyota City, Japan; client, City of Toyota City; architect, Taniguchi and Associates

ASLA Merit Award (California Council): Martin Luther King Jr. Promenade and Civic Park, San Diego, California; client, Center City Development Corporation; urban designer, Austin Design Group

1996   ASLA Honor Award (Design): Nishi Harima Science Garden City, Hyogo Prefecture, Japan; client, Hyogo Prefecture Government and the Public Enterprise Agency; architects, Arata Isozaki and Associates and Tadao Ando and Associates

ASLA Honor Award (Design): Plaza Tower and Town Center Park, Costa Mesa, California; client, C. J. Segerstrom, Anton Boulevard Associates, and Orange County Performing Arts Center; architects, Cesar Pelli and Associates with CRRS

1995   ASLA Merit Award (Communication): *Invisible Gardens: The Search for Modernism in the American Landscape;* authors, Peter Walker and Melanie Simo

1994   ASLA Honor Award (Design): IBM Japan Makuhari, Makuhari, Chiba Prefecture, Japan; client, IBM Japan; architects, Taniguchi and Associates with Nihon Sekkei; associate landscape architect, Toshi-Keikan-Sekkei

ALSA Merit Award (Planning and Urban Design): Exposition Park Master Plan, Los Angeles, California; client, California Museum of Science and Industry; architect, Zimmer Gunsul Frasca Partnership

1993 ASLA National Classic Award: Foothill College, Los Altos Hills, California; architects, Ernest J. Kump and Associates and Masten and Hurd

ASLA Honor Award: IBM Solana, Westlake/Southlake, Texas; client, Maguire/Thomas Partnership and IBM Corporation; architects, Mitchell/Giurgola and Ricardo Legoretta Arquitectos

AIA Urban Design Award of Excellence: Exposition Park Master Plan, Los Angeles, California; client, California Museum of Science and Industry; architect, Zimmer Gunsul Frasca Partnership

1992 AIA Institute Honor to Peter Walker for his work in contemporary landscape architecture

Gold Medal, Second Biennial of Mexican Architecture: IBM Solana, Westlake/Southlake, Texas; client, Maguire/Thomas Partnership and IBM Corporation; architect, Ricardo Legorreta Arquitectos

1991 ASLA San Diego Chapter President's Award of Excellence: Martin Luther King Jr. Promenade, San Diego, California; client, Center City Development Corporation

ASLA Merit Award: Marina Linear Park, San Diego, California; client, Center City Development Corporation

Twenty Year Design Award, City of Menlo Park: Sharon Green Apartments; client, Lincoln Properties; architect, Crosby, Thorton Hill Associates

1990 Twentieth Urban Beautification Award, "New Commercial Landscape," Los Angeles Business Council: The Santa Monica Five Parking Structure, Santa Monica, California; client, City of Santa Monica; architect, Johnson and Fein

ASLA Merit Award: IBM Solana Arrivals Garden and Village Center, Westlake, Texas

1988 ASLA Merit Award: Office Development and Village Center, IBM Solana, Westlake/Southlake, Texas; client: Maguire/Thomas Partnership and IBM Corporation; architects, Mitchel/Giurgola and Ricardo Legorreta Arquitectos

ASLA Merit Award: Roof Garden, 190 Marlborough Street, Boston, Massachusetts, with Martha Schwartz and John Wong

ASLA Merit Award: "Six Views: Contemporary Landscape Architecture," California State College, Fullerton, California; exhibition and catalogue by Dextra Frankel and Pamela Burton

Center City Development Corporation Competition, First Prize: Marina Linear Park, San Diego, California; artists, Andrea Blum and Dennis Adams, with Austin Design Group and Church Engineering

Eleventh North American Prairie Conference Landscape Design Award: Office Development and Village Center, IBM Solana, Westlake/Southlake, Texas; client, Maguire/Thomas Partnership and IBM Corporation; architects, Mitchell/Giurgola and Ricardo Legorreta Arquitectos

1987 ASLA Honor Award: Tanner Fountain, Cambridge, Massachusetts, with The SWA Group, Richard Chaix, and sculptor Joan Brigham; client, Harvard University

ASLA Merit Award: Concord Performing Arts Center, Concord, California; client, City of Concord; architect, Frank Gehry and Associates

ASLA Merit Award: Sidney Walton Park, San Francisco, California; client, Golden Gateway/San Francisco Redevelopment Agency

San Francisco Landscape Garden Show Merit Award: Garden entitled "We Know How Burgers Should Be!" San Francisco, California

1986 ASLA Texas Chapter Merit Award: Burnett Park, Fort Worth, Texas

Los Angeles Beautiful Ten-Year Maintenance Award: Security Pacific National Bank Plaza, Los Angeles, California; architect, Albert C. Martin and Associates

1985 ASLA New England Chapter Award of Excellence: Burnett Park, Fort Worth, Texas; clients, City of Fort Worth and Charles Tandy Foundation

ASLA New England Chapter Merit Award: Cambridge Center Roof Garden, Cambridge, Massachusetts, with The SWA Group; client, Boston Properties; architect, Moshe Safdie and Associates

ASLA New England Chapter Merit Award: Tanner Fountain, Cambridge, Massachusetts, with The SWA Group, Richard Chaix, and sculptor Joan Brigham; client, Harvard University

ASLA Northern California Chapter Honor Award: Sidney Walton Park, San Francisco, California; client, Golden Gateway/San Francisco Redevelopment Agency

1984 ASLA Merit Award: Cambridge Center Roof Garden, Cambridge, Massachusetts, with The SWA Group; client, Boston Properties; architect, Moshe Safdie and Associates

ASLA New England Chapter Honor Award: Promontory Point, Newport Beach, California; client, The Irvine Company; architect, Fisher-Friedman Associates

ASLA New England Chapter Honor Award: Weyerhaeuser Corporate Headquarters, Tacoma, Washington; client, Weyerhaeuser Company; architect, Skidmore, Owings & Merrill

ASLA New England Chapter Merit Award: Ohlone College, Fremont, California; architect, Ernest J. Kump and Associates

ASLA Northern California Chapter Honor Award: Concord Performing Arts Center, Concord, California; client, City of Concord; architect, Frank Gehry and Associates

ASLA Northern California Chapter Merit Award: Elkhorn Valley Resort, Sun Valley, Idaho; client, Sun Valley Company; architect, Killingsworth, Brady & Associates

ASLA Southern California Chapter Merit Award: Woodbridge (New Community) Master Plan, Irvine, California; client, The Irvine Company

1983 ASLA Honor Award: Herman Miller, Rockland, California; client, Herman Miller, Inc.; architects, Frank Gehry and Associates, Dreyfuss and Blackford, and Stanley Tigerman

ASLA Merit Award: Burnett Park, Fort Worth, Texas

ASLA Merit Award: IBM Clearlake, Houston, Texas; client, IBM Corporation; architect, CRSS

AIA California Chapter Honor Award: Columbus City Hall, Columbus, Indiana; client, City of Columbus; architect, Skidmore, Owings & Merrill

1980 California Garden Club, Landscape Architectural Award of Merit: Security Pacific National Bank Plaza, Los Angeles, California; client, SPNB; architect, Albert C. Martin & Associates

AIA Santa Clara Valley Chapter, Special Commendation for Excellence in Design: Foothill College, Los Altos Hills, California; architects, Ernest J. Kump and Associates and Masten and Hurd

1979 American Association of Nurserymen National Landscape Award: Security Pacific National Bank Plaza, Los Angeles, California; client, SPNB; architect, Albert C. Martin & Associates

Architectural Record Award of Excellence: The Village of Loon Mountain, Lincoln, New Hampshire; client, Loon Mountain Development Company; architect, Huygens and Tappe

1978 California Landscape Contractors Sweepstakes Award: IBM Santa Teresa Laboratory, Santa Teresa, California; client, IBM Corporation; architect, MBT Associates

1977 AIA Honor Award: Concord Performing Arts Center, Concord, California; client, City of Concord; architect, Frank Gehry and Associates

AIA Honor Award: IBM West Coast Programming Center, Santa Teresa, California; client, IBM Corporation; architect, MBT Associates

Pacific Coast Builders Conference Golden Nugget Merit Award: Woodbridge (New Community), Irvine, California; client, The Irvine Company; architect, Fisher-Friedman Associates

U.S. Department of Housing and Urban Development Design Concept Honor Award: Concord Performing Arts Center, Concord, California; client, City of Concord; architect, Frank Gehry and Associates

1976 U.S. Department of Housing and Urban Development Design Concept Honor Award: Buchanan Street Mall, San Francisco, California; client, San Francisco Redevelopment Agency

AIP Certificate of Merit: The San Diego Unified Port District, Embarcadero Development Plan, San Diego, California; client, City of San Diego

1975 AIA Honor Award: Cedar Square West, Minneapolis, Minnesota; architects, Ralph Rapson and Associates and Gingold-Pink Architecture; planners, Arton Aschman Associates

AIA/House and Home First Honor Award: Ethan's Glen, Houston, Texas; cient, Gerald D. Hines Interests; architect, Fisher-Friedman Associates

AIA/House and Home First Honor Award: Promontory Point, Newport Beach, California; client, The Irvine Company; architect, Fisher-Friedman Associates

AIA Central States Region Award of Excellence: Johnson County Community College, Kansas City, Kansas; architect, Marshall and Brown

AIA Kansas City Chapter, Merit Award: Penn Valley Community College, Kansas City, Missouri; architect, Marshall and Brown

American Association of School Administrators Special Citation: Johnson County Community College, Kansas City, Kansas; architect, Marshall and Brown

American Association of School Administrators Special Citation: Penn Valley Community College, Kansas City, Missouri; architect, Marshall and Brown

U.S Department of Housing and Urban Development Honor Award: Cedar Square West, Minneapolis, Minnesota; architects, Ralph Rapson and Associates and Gingold-Pink Architecture; planners, Barton Aschman Associates

1974 U.S. Department of Housing and Urban Development Design Concept Honor Award: Works of art, Golden Gateway, San Francisco, California; architects, Wurster, Bernardi & Emmons, De Mars and Reay, Pietro Belluschi and Milton Schwartz, Skidmore, Owings & Merrill; artists, François Stahly, Aris Demetrios, Jacques Overhof, Seymour Lipton, Henry Moore, Mario Marraini, Charles Perry

1973 California Landscape Contractors Sweepstakes Award: Sears Roebuck Western Regional Headquarters Building, Alhambra, California; client, Sears Roebuck; architect, Albert C. Martin & Associates

AIA Collaborative Achievement Award: In conjunction with other team members, for the San Francisco Bay Area Rapid Transit System, San Francisco, California

1972 U.S. Federal Housing Authority and SPUR (San Francisco Planning and Urban Renewal Association) John L. Merrill Honor Award: Pedestrian ways, Golden Gateway, San Francisco, California; architects, Wurster, Bernardi & Emmons and De Mars and Reay

Omaha Chamber of Commerce Award: Regency Lake and Tennis Club, Omaha, Nebraska; client, Mutual of Omaha; architect, Leo A. Daly Company

ASLA Merit Award: Carmel Valley Manor, Carmel Valley, California; client, Northern California Congregational Retirement Home, Inc.; architect, Skidmore, Owings & Merrill

ASLA Merit Award: Crocker Plaza, San Francisco, California; client, Crocker Bank; architect, Welton Becket & Associates

ASLA Merit Award: Foothill College, Los Altos Hills, California; architects, Ernest J. Kump and Associates and Masten and Hurd

ASLA Merit Award: Weyerhaeuser Corporate Headquarters, Tacoma, Washington; client, Weyerhaeuser Company; architect, Skidmore, Owings & Merrill

AIA Honor Award/Bartlett Award: Weyerhaeuser Corporate Headquarters, Tacoma, Washington; client, Weyerhaeuser Company; architect, Skidmore, Owings & Merrill

1971 AIA/House and Home Merit Award: Mariner Square, Newport Beach, California; client, The Irvine Company; architect, Fisher-Friedman Associates

AIP California Chapter, Northern Section, Merit Award: Steinberger Neighborhood, Redwood Shores, Redwood City, California; client, Leslie Properties

San Francisco Society Awards Certificate: Cochiti Lake, New Mexico; client, Cochiti Indian Council; architect, Frank Gehry and Associates

ASLA Honor Award: Mariner Square, Newport Beach, California; client, The Irvine Company; architect, Fisher-Friedman Associates

ASLA Merit Award: Bay Area Rapid Transit District Linear Park, Albany-El Cerrito, California

ASLA Merit Award: Fashion Island Shopping Center, Newport Beach, California; client, The Irvine Company; architects, Welton Becket Associates and William Pereira

ASLA Merit Award: Upjohn Corporation World Headquarters, Kalamazoo, Michigan; client, Upjohn Corporation; architect, Bruce Graham, Skidmore, Owings & Merrill

Architectural Record Award of Excellence: Mariner Square, Newport Beach California; client, The Irvine Company; architect, Fisher-Friedman Associates

California Landscape Contractors Award for Design Excellence: Alza Corporation, Palo Alto, California; architect, McCue, Boone, Tomsick

1970 U.S. Department of Housing and Urban Development Design Excellence Award: Diamond Heights Housing, San Francisco, California; architects, Nobler and Chen and Karl Treffinger

City of Menlo Park Design Award: Sharon Green Apartments, Menlo Park, California; client, Lincoln Properties; architect, Crosby, Thorton Hill Associates

1968 ASLA Merit Award: Golden Gateway Redevelopment, San Francisco, California; architects, Wurster, Bernardi and Emmons, De Mars and Reay, Pietro Belluschi and Milton Schwartz, and Skidmore, Owings & Merrill

U.S Department of Housing and Urban Development Merit Award: Bay Area Rapid Transit District Linear Park, Albany-El Cerrito, California

1966 U.S Department of Housing and Urban Development Merit Award: Westmont College Dormitories, Santa Barbara, California; architect, Neil Smith

1964 U.S. Federal Housing Authority Honor Award: Carmel Valley Manor, Carmel Valley, California; client, Northern California Congregational Retirement Home, Inc.; architect, Skidmore, Owings & Merrill

U.S Federal Housing Authority Honor Award: The Sequoias, Portola Valley, California; client, Northern California Presbyterian Home, Inc.; architect, Skidmore, Owings & Merrill

1963 AIA First Honor Award/The American Library Association and the National Book Committee: The Edward Clark Grosset Library, Bennington College, Bennington, Vermont; architects, Carl Koch and Associates and Pietro Belluschi

AIA First Honor Award: Los Gatos Civic Center, Los Gatos, California; architect, Stickney and Hull

1962 Architectural League of New York, Collaborative Medal of Honor: Thomas J. Watson Research Center, Yorktown Heights, New York; client, IBM Corporation; architect, Eero Saarinen and Associates

AIA First Honor Award: Foothill College, Los Altos Hills, California; architects, Ernest J. Kump and Associates and Masten and Hurd

1960 *Progressive Architecture* Design Award: Foothill College, Los Altos Hills, California; architects, Ernest J. Kump and Associates and Masten and Hurd

Partner Résumés

Peter Walker, FASLA, Senior Partner

Education
Harvard University Graduate School of Design,
    Master of Landscape Architecture, 1957 (Weidenman Prize)
University of Illinois, graduate study in landscape architecture, 1956
University of California at Berkeley,
    Bachelor of Science in Landscape Architecture, 1955

Professional Experience
Peter Walker and Partners (Chairman of the Board), Berkeley, California
Peter Walker William Johnson and Partners, Berkeley, California
The SWA Group, Sausalito, California
Sasaki, Walker Associates, Inc., San Francisco, California
Hideo Sasaki & Associates, Watertown, Massachusetts
Landscape Architects Associates, Champaign-Urbana, Illinois
Lawrence Halprin, Landscape Architects, San Francisco, California

Teaching
Chairman, Department of Landscape Architecture,
    University of California at Berkeley, 1997-1999
Charles Eliot Chair, Harvard University Graduate School of Design, 1992
Editorial Board, *Landscape Architecture*, 1988-1991
Adjunct Professor, Harvard University Graduate School of Design,
    1976–1991
Chairman, Department of Landscape Architecture, Harvard University
    Graduate School of Design,1978–1981
Acting Director, Urban Design Program, Harvard University Graduate
    School of Design, 1977–1978
Visiting Critic, Massachusetts Institute of Technology, 1959
Instructor in Landscape Architecture, Harvard University Graduate School
    of Design, 1958–1959

Guest Lecturer / Visiting Critic
Ball State University, Collegi d'Arquitectes de Cataluyna, Florida State
University; Illinois Institute of Technology, Iowa State University, Louisiana
State University, Ohio State University, Pennsylvania State University,
Rapperswile Summer Academy in Switzerland, Universidad Menendez-
Palayo, University of California at Berkeley, University of California at
Davis, University of California at Los Angeles, University of Colorado,
University of Illinois, University of Kansas, University of Massachusetts,
University of Michigan, University of New Mexico, University of North
Carolina, University of Pennsylvania, University of Southern California,
University of Taiwan, University of Virginia, University of Washington,
Washington University, Yale University

Speaker
Dumbarton Oaks, 2003; Contemporary European Design Conference,
Harvard, 2001; Canal Isabel II 150th Anniversary Seminar, Madrid,
2001; 100th Anniversary of the GSD, 2000; Sasaki Years at Harvard
Conference, 1999; International Landscape Forum, Fukushima Prefecture,
Japan, 1999; IFLA World Congress, Bali, 1998; IFLA, Buenos Aires,
1997; James Rose Lecture Series, University of Massachusetts, 1997;

International Symposium on Asia Pacific Architecture, Hawaii, 1997;
Korean Institute of Landscape Architects, 1997; Australian Institute of
Landscape Architects, 1997; Preserving Contemporary Landscape
Architecture Conference, Wave Hill, New York, 1995; Escondido
Museum of Art, 1995; Third International Symposium of Architects,
Mexico, 1994; IFLA, Mexico City, 1994; Monterey Design Conference,
1993; Municipal Art Society, New York City, 1992; IFLA, Singapore,
1991; Kajima/GSD Conference, Tokyo, Japan, 1989; and IFLA,
Boston, 1988

Honors
The ASLA Gold Medal, 2004
Thomas Jefferson Medal, University of Virginia, 2004
Centennial Medal, Harvard University, 2003
Distinguished Alumni Award, University of California at Berkeley, 2003
John R. Bracken Medal, Pennsylvania State University, 2003
Honorary Doctorate of Landscape Architecture, University of Pretoria,
    South Africa, 2003
Institute Honor, American Institute of Architects, 1992
Resident, American Academy in Rome, 1991
Fellow, American Society of Landscape Architects
Fellow, Institute for Urban Design

Competitions
World Trade Center Memorial, with Michael Arad, 2004; Novartis
Campus, Basel, Switzerland, 1999; Saitama Plaza, Saitama Prefecture,
Japan, 1995; Industrial and Commercial Bank of China, Beijing, China,
1993; T. F. Green Airport, Warwick, Rhode Island, 1993; Sony Center,
Berlin, Germany, 1992; Federal Triangle, Washington, D.C., 1990;
San Diego Marina Linear Park, California, 1988.

Design Juries
Mission Bay Site Master Plan Competition, San Francisco; American
Institute of Architects; American Society of Landscape Architects; Prince of
Wales Prize in Urban Design; American Academy in Rome, Landscape
Architecture; National Endowment for the Arts, First Collaborative Awards
Jury; Progressive Architecture Urban Design Awards; and National
Building Museum Honor Awards

Douglas Ross Findlay, Senior Partner

Education
Harvard University Graduate School of Design
    Master of Landscape Architecture with Distinction, 1984
California State Polytechnic University, Pomona
    Bachelor of Science in Landscape Architecture, 1980
Rio Hondo College, 1976

Professional Experience
Peter Walker and Partners (Partner in Charge), Berkeley, California
Douglas Ross Findlay Landscape Architect, Cambridge, Massachusetts
Michael Van Valkenburg Associates, Cambridge, Massachusetts
The SWA Group (Associate), Sausalito, California

Awards

Charles Eliot Traveling Fellowship, 1984
Rome Prize Finalist, American Academy in Rome, 1984
Janet D. Webel Scholarship Prize, 1983
ASLA National Distinguished Student Award, 1981
Gamma Sigma Delta Honors, 1980
ASLA Certificate of Honor, 1980
Jack Evans Design Scholarship, 1977
Kawasaki Design Award, 1976

Teaching

Guest juror in Landscape Architecture, Harvard University, Radcliffe College
Visiting teaching assistant in Landscape Architecture, Harvard University
    Graduate School of Design

Speaker

ASLA Texas Chapter, Cal Poly Pomona Alumni Lecture, Nevada State
Chamber of Commerce

Paul Sieron, Partner

Education

University of Michigan
    Master of Landscape Architecture, 1981
University of Michigan
    Bachelor of Science, 1978

Professional Experience

Peter Walker and Partners (Senior Project Manager), Berkeley, California
William J. Johnson Associates, Inc., Ann Arbor, Michigan
B.J.R., Inc., Ann Arbor, Michigan
Skidmore, Owings & Merrill, Chicago, Illinois

Teaching

Instructor, University of Michigan

Tony K. Sinkosky, Construction Partner

Education

University of Illinois, Bachelor of Landscape Architecture, 1978
San Francisco Center for Architecture and Urban Studies, 1977

Professional Experience

Peter Walker and Partners (Principal in Charge of Construction Documents
    and Construction Observation), Berkeley, California
Hargreaves, Allen, Sinkosky & Loomis (Partner), San Francisco, California
The SWA Group (Associate), Laguna Beach and Sausalito, California

Memberships

American Society for Testing Materials
California Native Grass Association
Construction Specifications Institute
International Erosion Control Association
International Society of Arboriculture

David Walker, Design Partner

Education

Harvard University Graduate School of Design
    Master of Landscape Architecture with Distinction, 1992
Rhode Island School of Design
    Bachelor of Fine Arts in Landscape Architecture with Honors, 1983

Professional Experience

Peter Walker and Partners, Berkeley, California
P.O.D., Inc., San Francisco, California
William D. Warner, Architects and Planners, Providence, Rhode Island
Searle & Searle Landscape Architects and Planners,
    Providence, Rhode Island

Awards

ASLA Certificate of Honor, 1992
Harwood Fund Prize, 1983

Published Photographic Work

Land Forum, 1996
Process Architecture 118, 1994
Landscape Architecture Magazine,
    Visionary Landscapes Competition,1993
Peter Walker, 1990
Process Architecture 85, Japan 1989
Architectural Review, England, September 1989
Southern Landscape Architecture, September 1989
Landscape Architecture, October–November 1989
Progressive Architecture, 1989
S.D. Magazine, 1988
"Six Views," *Contemporary Landscape Architecture,* 1986

Jane G. Williamson, Partner

Education

University of California at Berkeley, courses in business law, management
accounting, construction management, and history of landscape
architecture, 1980, 1983, 1985-1986
Stafford Hall School of Business, 1977

Experience

Peter Walker and Partners (Senior Partner, Business Systems),
    Berkeley, California
Samwhan Corporation, San Francisco, California

Current PWP Employees

Carmen Arroyo
Daniel Baur
Janet Beagle
Kari Boeskov
Paul Buchanan
Shanai Chung
April Deerr
Matthew Donham

Kathryn Drinkhouse
Daphne Edwards
Liz Einwiller, Associate
Doug Findlay, Partner
Annette Flores
Jane Gillette
Adam Greenspan,
  Associate
Jim Grimes, Associate

Claudia Harari
Sandy Harris, Associate
Jennifer Henry
Kazunari Kobayashi
Sarah Kuehl, Associate
James A. Lord, Associate
Gilat Lovinger
Gabriel Meil
Moritz Moellers

Susan Pinto
A. J. Pires
Taya Rhodes
Cornelia Roppel
Doris Schenk, Associate
Paul Sieron, Partner
Tony Sinkosky, Partner
Kelly Spokus
Gisela Steber, Associate

Jeffrey Ulm
David Walker, Partner
Peter Walker, Partner
Matthias Wehrle
Christian Werthmann,
  Associate
Timothy Wight
JaneWilliamson, Partner
Wan-chih Yin

**PWP Employees
1984–Present**

Steven Abrahams
Branden Adams
Wolfgang Aichele
Verda Alexandra
Duncan Alford
Annie Amundsen
Kira Applehans
Sierra Bainbridge
C. Timothy Baird
Ka-t Bakhu
Alec Balliet
Arthur Bartenstein
John Bela
Katherine Bennett
Eva Bernhard
Cathy Deino Blake, Partner
Claire Bobrow
Michelle Bond
Theodore Booth
Charles Brandau
Kimberly Brigati
Annegret Brinkschulte
Jennifer Brooke, Associate
Michael J. Brooks, Partner
Carl Brown
Caroline Burzan
Dixi Carrillo
Juliana Carvalho Do Val
Elizabeth Chaffin
Alexandre Champagne
Conway Chang
Sara Chisum
Ana Coello
Philippe Coignet
Steel Colony
David Condron
April Cottini
Jennifer Cox
Gina Crandell
James Curtis
Andrew Day
Yasmin Del Rio
John Dennis

Kimberlee De Jong
Albert DeSilver
Christine Dianni
James Dinh
Nadine Dreyer
Michelle Dubin
Sara Fairchild
Andrew Findlay
Nicole Findlay
Nancy Finley
Andreas Flache
Raeven Flores
Martha Folger
Joanna Fong
Anna Forrester
Ron Frank
Philip Frankl
Marta Fry
Yoriko Fukushi
Thomas (Russ) Gage
Charles Gamez
Lisa Ganucheau
Alke Gerdes
Liette Gilbert
Robert Gilmore
Marshall Gold
Elizabeth Gourley
Megan Griscom
Anne Guillebeaux
E. Leesa Hager
James Haig Streeter
Karolos Hanikian
Jane Hansen
Tim Harvey
Robert Hewitt
Chester Hill
Martin Hoffman
Martin Holland
Roxanne Holt
Hermes Illana
Dorothée Imbert
Christine Jepson
Laura Jerrard
Bruce Jett
Dirk Johnson

Mark Johnson
William Johnson, Partner
Rachel Johnson
David Jung
Raphael Justewicz
Martin Kamph
Akshay Kaul
Ken Kawai
Tatsuya Kawashima
Esther Kerkmann
Rhonda Killian
Elizabeth Krason
Benjamin Kuchinsky
Matei Kucina
Denise Kupperman
Sonja Kurhanewicz
Grace Kwak
Shelby LaMotte
Patrick Lando
Nicolas Lantz
Tom Leader, Partner
Paul Lee
Terence Lee
Ihsien Lee
Mark Lehmann
Mia Lehrer, Partner
Randy Lein
Christian Lemon
Christopher Leong
Carol Lesh
Leah Levy
Jaruvan Li
Qindong Liang
Lynda Lim
Leor Lovinger
Henry Lu
David Madison
Elliott Maltby
Mark Maniaci
Esther Margulies
Anuradha Mathur
Phoebe McCormick
Kitty McDaniel
Alex Mena
David Meyer, Partner

Kirsten Miller
Javier Miranda
Yasuhiko Mitani
Toru Mitani
Kjersti Monson
Cary Moon
Duane Moore
Julie Morris
Christian Mueller
Shuichi Murakami
Mary Muszynski
Kevin Napoli
Susan Nettlebeck
Diane Nickelsberg
Makoto Noborisaka
Joseph Nootbaar
Hans Oerlemans
Michael Oser
Peter Osler
Mignon O'Young
Sally Pagliai
Pamela Palmer
Jose Parral
Joaquin Pedrin
Jacob Petersen
Johanna Phelps
Laura Phipps
Marty Poirier
Marie Rafalko
Scott Rahder
Gustavo Ramirez
Lawrence Reed
Sandra Reed
Elizabeth Reifeiss
Ellen Reihsaus
Martin Rein-Cano
Kerry Ricketts
Dee Rizor
Isabel Robertson
Robert Rock
Maura Rockcastle
Denise Rogers
Robert Rombold
Melody Rose
Lisa Roth

Gabriel Rustini
Matthew Safly
Michael Sanchez
Christopher Scavone
Kim Schumacher
Martha Schwartz
Nina Seelos
Joon Seo Park
Christopher Sherwin
Heidi Siegmund
Ramsey Silberberg
Lucia E.Silva
Carina Simmchen
Melanie Simo
Jeffrey Smith
Ken Smith
Carol Souza
Angelika Spies
Kim Stryker
Margaret Stueve
Bryan Suchy
Kendra Taylor
Jane Tesner
Eric Thomasson
Gina Thornton
John Threadgill
Randy Thueme
John Tornes
Maria Toscano
James Trulove, Partner
Christian Tschumi
Ludwing Vaca
Sarah Vance, Partner
Christopher Varesi
Nicholas Wessel
Stella Wirk
Aichele Wolfgang
Lauren Wong
Robert Wood
Kathryn Woods
Mei Wu
Roderick Wyllie
Chris Yates
Anna Liza Ybarra
Michael Zonta

230

Photography

Tom Adams
24

Paul Buchanan
160

Gerry Campbell
14, 15, 20, 21,
25

Dixi Carillo
12, 13, 16, 17,
18, 28, 30, 31,
37, 198

Doug Findlay
61, 63, 65, 82

Tom Fox
24

Jim Grimes
91

Tim Harvey
65, 70, 74, 79,
89, 106, 108,
109,152, 173

Jim Hedrich
29

Kazuaki
Hosokawa
80, 81, 87

Tim Hursley
131, 132, 133,
135

Eric Keune of
Skidmore, Owings
& Merrill
142

Susumu Koshimizu
40

Tom Leader
33

James A. Lord
55, 72, 73, 75,
114, 117, 153,
174, 175,
184,186, 188,
193, 201, 214

Courtesy of the
Lower Manhattan
Development
Corporation,
Copyright 2004
LMDC; rendering
by dbox
163, 164, 166,
167

David Meyer
26, 39

Hiko Mitani
34

Atsushi Nakamichi
38, 39

Courtesy of
Novartis
190

Erik-Jan Ouwerkerk
92, 93

Pamela Palmer
31, 121

Dean Perry
135

Doris Schenk
153

Kelly Spokus
154

Courtesy of the
Sydney Olympic
Park Authority
82, 184

Hiroshi Tonaka
34, 35, 41, 83,
84, 85, 86, 122

David Walker
13, 23, 26, 41,
98, 99, 101,
148, 188, 194,
195, 197, 216

Peter Walker
12, 17, 27, 40,
63, 64, 65, 77,
78, 117, 119,
122, 140, 170,
180, 184,

Alan Ward
22, 24

Christian
Werthmann
127, 154

Matthias Wehrle
196, 197

Tim Wight
6, 7, 14, 15, 18,
19, 30, 31, 44,
45, 46, 47, 48,
49, 50, 51, 52,
53, 54, 56, 57,
66, 68, 69, 3,
34, 95, 97, 104,
105, 110, 111,
113, 115, 117,
118, 126, 127,
128, 129, 130,
132, 134,135,
136, 137, 152,
153, 195, 214,
foldouts 4 and 5

Eiji Yonekura
32

Drawings

Chris Grubbs
152, 158, 159,
171, 176, 177,
178, 179, 187,
189, 206, 207,
213, 215, 219,
foldouts 12
and 13

William Johnson
181

Machado & Silvetti
Associates in
association with Olin
Partnership
151

Courtesy of National
Capital Planning
Commission
202-203, 204-205,
206-207

Bob Wood
124, 125